Family Circle
Christmas
CRAFTS

Family Circle Christmas CRAFTS

HAMLYN

First published in Great Britain in 1993 by
Hamlyn
an imprint of Reed Consumer Books Limited
Michelin House, 81 Fulham Road
London SW3 6RB
and Auckland, Melbourne, Singapore and Toronto

Editor: **Catherine Ward**
Art Editor: **Prue Bucknall**
Executive Editor: **Judith More**
Art Director: **Jacqui Small**

This product is suitable for ages 14 years upwards. We
recommend that children under the age of 14 years should
be supervised by an adult.

Not suitable for children under 36 months.

ISBN: 0 60058 033 4

Typeset by Dorchester Typesetting Group Ltd,
Dorchester, Dorset
Origination by Mandarin Offset, Singapore
Printed and Bound in Great Britain by Severn Valley Press

CONTENTS

To Tom
A Very Merry
Christmas
love
Rwth xxx

EDIBLE GIFTS

CHRISTMAS IS THE BEST TIME OF YEAR FOR "FOODIES". HERE WE'VE INCLUDED SOME OF OUR FAVOURITE FAMILY CIRCLE RECIPES THAT TRADITIONALLY PUT IN A GUEST APPEARANCE DURING THE FESTIVE SEASON. NOTHING CAN BEAT A FRESHLY MADE BATCH OF HOME-MADE SWEETS OR SAVOURIES AND, SINCE YOU'RE TAKING THE TROUBLE TO MAKE THEM, IT'S JUST AS EASY TO WHIZ UP A DOZEN EXTRA FOR A SUPPLY TO TREAT THE FAMILY AND TO SURPRISE FRIENDS AND NEIGHBOURS. MAKE UP QUANTITIES AND BAG THEM IN CLEAR CELLOPHANE TIED WITH RIBBONS OR CHOOSE A SELECTION TO PUT IN SWEET CASES AND HEAP INTO BOXES THAT YOU'VE PREPARED YOURSELF BY COVERING IN GIFTWRAP.

SHORTBREAD

Makes 8 wedges or 12 fingers
100g (4oz) unsalted butter
50g (2oz) caster sugar
225g (8oz) plain flour, sifted

1 Beat the butter until it is very soft, then work in the sugar with your hand, followed by the sifted flour.

2 Roll out the mixture on a lightly floured surface to an 18cm (7in) round and mark into wedges, or roll out to a 1cm (½in) thick rectangle and cut into fingers. Put the shapes onto a baking sheet and prick them all over with a fork.

3 Cook at 150°C (300°F/ Gas 2) for 30-40 minutes, or until pale golden.

4 Leave to cool for 2 minutes. If you are making wedges, mark into segments with a knife and leave to set for 5 minutes. Put on a wire rack to cool.

any froth from the surface, then pour it over the pâté to cover completely.

3 Before the butter sets, garnish with green and red peppers, cut as holly leaves and berries. Chill well before serving.

COCONUT ICE

Makes 2.25kg (5lb)
1.8kg (4lb) granulated sugar
450g (1lb) coarse-cut desiccated coconut
600ml (1pt) water
Red food colouring

1 Put half the sugar and ½pt (300ml) water into a heavy saucepan and heat gently until the sugar has completely dissolved. Bring the mixture to the boil and heat to 115°C (239°F) on a sugar thermometer, or until a spoonful of the mixture forms a soft ball when dropped into cold water.

2 Remove from the heat and add half the coconut. Stir until thick, then press into an oiled 30.5 × 15 × 3.8cm (12 × 6 × 1½in) tin.

3 Repeat step 1 with the remaining sugar. Remove the pan from the heat and add the remaining coconut, together with a couple of drops of red food colouring. Stir the mixture until thick, then press it down on top of the white coconut ice. Leave to cool and set, then cut into squares.

LEMON CURD

Makes 900g (2lb)
4 lemons, grated rind and juice
4 eggs, beaten
100g (4oz) butter
450g (1lb) granulated sugar

1 Put all the ingredients into the top of a double saucepan or a bowl set over simmering water. Stir until the sugar dissolves.

2 Continue cooking, stirring occasionally, until thick.

3 Strain the curd and ladle into warm, clean jars. Leave to cool, then seal and label the jars. You can store lemon curd for up to 2 months.

food FOR THOUGHT

FUDGE

Makes 1.1kg (2¼lb)
100g (4oz) unsalted butter
397g (14oz) can full-cream sweetened condensed milk
450g (1lb) demerara sugar

1 Place the butter and the full-cream condensed milk in a saucepan and cook over a gentle heat until the butter has melted. Stir in the sugar and cook over a medium heat until the mixture reaches 115°C (239°F) on a

sugar thermometer, or until the "soft ball" stage (i.e. when a spoonful of the mixture forms a soft ball when it is dropped into a cup of cold water).

2 Remove the pan from the heat and beat the mixture well. Pour into a buttered 30.5 × 15 × 2.5cm (12 × 6 × 1in) tin. Leave to set slightly, then cut into squares before the fudge becomes too cold and more difficult to divide.

STILTON PÂTÉ

Makes 325g (12oz)
225g (8oz) blue stilton, crumbled
100g (4oz) unsalted butter
2tbsp brandy
2tbsp single or double cream
Green and red pepper to garnish

1 Mash the stilton with half the butter and all the brandy and cream together until smooth.

2 Press the mixture into a 300ml (½pt) pâté dish. Melt the remaining butter. Skim off

CHOCOLATE-CHIP COOKIES

Makes 15

100g (4oz) butter
100g (4oz) granulated sugar
100g (4oz) soft, light-brown
  sugar
1 egg
1tsp vanilla essence
100g (4oz) wholewheat flour,
  sifted
100g (4oz) self-raising flour,
  sifted
150g (6oz) chopped, plain dark
  chocolate

1 Cream the butter with the sugars, then beat in the egg a little at a time with the vanilla essence. Combine the flours in a separate bowl and stir them into the mixture, followed by the chopped plain dark-chocolate chips. Mix well.

2 Spoon the mixture onto a lightly greased baking tray – you should have enough to make 15 biscuits. Flatten the tops slightly. Cook at 190°C (375°F/Gas 5) for 8-10 minutes. Leave to cool.

FOR THE TREE

Makes 20-24

225g (8oz) plain flour
25g (1oz) cornflour
150g (6oz) softened butter
100g (4oz) caster sugar
1tbsp ground ginger
100g (4oz) icing sugar
Gold and silver food paint

1 Beat together the flour, cornflour, butter, caster sugar and ginger to form a soft dough. Roll out the mixture to 6mm (¼in) on a lightly floured surface and cut out shapes using pastry cutters.

2 Place the shapes on a greased baking sheet and use a skewer to make a hole in each for attaching the ribbon.

3 Bake at 180°C (350°F/Gas 4) for 10-12 minutes, or until golden. Leave to cool.

4 Mix the icing sugar with enough water to form a thick paste and use this to ice the shapes. When the icing is dry, paint on the features using metallic food paint. Finally thread with ribbon. Note: some brands of food paint are inedible so check the label before use.

MINI CHRISTMAS CAKES

Makes 6

FOR THE CAKES:
6 × 225g (8oz) cans, emptied
150g (6oz) butter
100g (4oz) soft dark-brown
  sugar
4 eggs, beaten

200g (7oz) plain flour
1tsp mixed spice
225g (8oz) currants
150g (6oz) raisins
100g (4oz) sultanas
75g (3oz) dried apricots
50g (2oz) blanched
  almonds, chopped
1 lemon

3tbsp orange juice
1 egg white
2tsp glycerine
450g (1lb) icing sugar
1tbsp apricot jam
100g (4oz) marzipan

TO FINISH:
6 small candles
Paper frill
Ribbon

1 Using a can opener, remove both ends from the six cans. Remove the contents, then wash, rinse and dry them thoroughly. Grease and line the sides, then place them on a greased and lined baking tray.

2 Cream the butter with the sugar until fluffy, then beat in the eggs a little at a time. Fold in the flour, mixed spice, dried fruit, almonds, grated lemon rind and orange juice.

3 Divide the mixture equally among the cans. Cook at 150°C (300°F/Gas 2) for 2 hours until golden. Leave the cakes to cool in their cans before turning them out onto a wire rack.

4 Put the egg white, 1tsp lemon juice and glycerine in a bowl. Gradually mix in the icing sugar. Cover with plastic kitchen film and set aside.

5 Warm the jam. Roll out the marzipan on a surface lightly dusted with icing sugar and cut out six 7.5cm (3in) rounds. Brush the cake tops with the warmed apricot jam and place a marzipan round on each. Spoon the icing on top of the cakes and swirl into snow peaks with a knife. Press a candle into the middle of each cake and decorate the sides with frilly paper and ribbon.

APRICOT CHEWS

Makes 32

225g (8oz) ready-to-eat dried apricots
4tbsp mixed nuts
75g (3oz) desiccated coconut
1 lemon
50g (2oz) angelica, chopped

1 Finely chop the apricots and nuts, then combine them with the coconut.

2 Grate the lemon rind and add to the apricot mixture with 1tsp lemon juice and the chopped angelica. Mix well or place in a food processor for a few seconds.

3 Tip the mixture out onto a board and roll into 32 balls.

4 Put into paper sweet cases.

WALNUT AND HONEY TRUFFLES

Makes 30

225g (8oz) walnut halves
100g (4oz) soft, light-brown sugar
2tbsp set honey
200g (7oz) plain chocolate
1tbsp vegetable oil

1 Reserve 30 complete walnut halves and then finely grind the rest in a food processor, rotary grater or nut mill.

2 Mix the ground nuts with the sugar and honey to form a thick paste, then roll into 30 balls.

3 Flatten the balls slightly and press a walnut half into each.

4 Melt the chocolate in a bowl set over simmering water, then stir in the oil.

5 Using a fork, dip each truffle into the melted chocolate. Shake off any excess chocolate and leave to set on non-stick baking paper.

6 Put into paper sweet cases.

CLOTTED-CREAM FUDGE

Makes 36

675g (1½lb) granulated sugar
100g (4oz) clotted cream
125ml (¼pt) milk
100g (4oz) maraschino cherries, quartered
Vanilla essence

1 Grease and base-line an 18cm (7in) square tin with non-stick baking paper.

2 Put the sugar, cream and milk into a heavy-based pan and heat gently, stirring occasionally, until the sugar has completely dissolved.

3 Bring the mixture to the boil and heat to 116°C (240°F) on a sugar thermometer. Add the cherries just before the fudge reaches the correct temperature.

4 Remove the pan from the heat and stir in a few drops of vanilla essence. Beat the fudge until it begins to thicken and starts to dry on the spoon.

5 Pour into the lined tin and spread evenly. Leave to cool slightly and cut into 36 squares with a sharp knife just before the fudge begins to set.

6 Wrap in twists of cellophane.

CHOCOLATE RUM 'N' RAISIN CUPS

Makes 20

50g (2oz) raisins
2tbsp rum
250g (9oz) white chocolate
125g (5oz) milk chocolate
65g (2½oz) unsalted butter
6tsp double cream

1 Put the raisins and rum into a bowl, cover and soak overnight.

2 Place 100g (4oz) of white chocolate in a bowl and melt over a pan of simmering water. Brush the chocolate thickly over the insides of 20 foil sweet cases. Turn them upside down and chill for 30 minutes.

3 In separate bowls, melt the remaining white chocolate and the milk chocolate over pans of simmering water. Stir half the butter into each. Stir 4tsp cream into the white chocolate and 2tsp cream into the milk chocolate. Leave to cool, stirring occasionally, until the mixtures hold soft peaks. Meanwhile, fill the chocolate sweet cases with the raisin mixture.

4 Spoon the white chocolate mixture into one side of a piping bag, fitted with a medium star nozzle, and the milk chocolate mixture into the other side. Pipe a swirl into each case. Chill.

ORANGE JELLIES

Makes 36

900g (2lb) granulated sugar
125ml (¼pt) water
225ml (8fl oz) concentrated orange juice
6tbsp gelatine
2tbsp orange liqueur
Granulated sugar for rolling

1 Put the sugar, water and 125ml (¼pt) orange juice into a heavy-based pan. Heat gently until the sugar has dissolved, stirring occasionally.

2 Bring the sugar syrup to the boil and heat without stirring to 116°C (240°F) on a sugar thermometer.

3 Sprinkle the gelatine evenly over the remaining orange juice and dissolve over a pan of hot water.

4 Stir the gelatine into the syrup, together with the liqueur, and pour into a damp 20cm (8in) square tin. Leave to set.

5 Turn the jelly out and cut into 36, 2.5cm (1in) shapes using a sharp knife. Roll in sugar to coat completely, then put into sweet cases.

sweet SUCCESS

CARAMEL MARSHMALLOW SLICES

Makes 24

100g (4oz) caramel toffees
25g (1oz) butter
1tbsp double cream
100g (4oz) icing sugar
75g (3oz) natural peanut kernels
75g (3oz) pink and white marshmallows, chopped
75g (3oz) desiccated coconut, toasted

1 Put the toffees, butter and cream into a pan and heat gently to melt. Stir in the sugar and nuts, mixing well. Finally, stir in the marshmallows a few pieces at a time.

2 Spoon the mixture onto a sheet of non-stick baking paper and shape into a "sausage" about 2.5cm (1in) in diameter. Roll in coconut.

3 Wrap in plastic kitchen film and chill until firm.

4 Cut into 24 slices. Wrap in twists of cellophane.

MARZIPAN CHERRIES

Makes 16

12 maraschino cherries
225g (8oz) white marzipan
Icing sugar for dusting

1 Drain the cherries and pat them dry with kitchen paper. Dust your worksurface with icing sugar and roll out the marzipan to a rectangle measuring 20.5 × 12.5cm (8 × 5in). Arrange the cherries in a line down the middle and wrap the marzipan around them.

2 Chill for 30 minutes, then cut into 16 slices. Serve in *petits-fours* cases.

SPICED NUTS

Makes 24

225g (8oz) blanched nuts (e.g. almonds, hazelnuts etc.)
2tbsp honey
2tbsp demerara sugar
15g (½oz) butter
½tsp ground ginger
½tsp mixed spice

1 Fry all the ingredients gently for 5 minutes, stirring occasionally.

2 When the nuts start popping, turn them onto a baking sheet to cool for 5 minutes. Spoon into *petits-fours* cases.

MARZIPAN MIXED FRUITS

Makes 16

225g (8oz) white marzipan
Green and red food colouring
Whole cloves
Caster sugar for dusting

1 To make apples, colour half the marzipan with green food colouring, then shape into apples.

2 To make the strawberries, colour the remaining marzipan red and then shape into strawberries. Make indentations in the sides by rolling the shapes against a fine nutmeg grater.

3 Dust the fruits with caster sugar and push a clove into the top of each. Serve in *petits-fours* cases. Note: the cloves should be discarded before eating.

CHOCOLATE BRAZILS

Makes 20

40 large, shelled Brazil nuts
50g (2oz) plain chocolate, melted
75g (3oz) white chocolate, melted

1 Coat 20 nuts in melted, dark chocolate and 20 in melted white chocolate. Press 2 nuts gently together.

2 Leave to cool, then put into *petits-fours* cases.

AFTER-DINNER MINT CHOCOLATES

Makes 16

75g (3oz) plain chocolate, melted
225g (8oz) icing sugar
1 egg white, lightly beaten
Peppermint essence
16 shelled hazelnuts

1 Brush the chocolate evenly over the insides of 16 *petits-fours* cases. Leave to chill.

2 Beat the sugar and egg white with a few drops of peppermint essence. Spoon all the mixture into the chilled cases.

3 Top each sweet with a hazelnut and decorate by drizzling any remaining chocolate over the top.

LEMON TWISTS

Makes 20

100g (4oz) ready-to-roll fondant icing
1 lemon
Yellow food colouring
Icing sugar for dusting

1 Knead the fondant icing with the lemon rind, 1tsp lemon juice and enough food colouring to make a pale-yellow colour. Add a little icing sugar if the mixture becomes too soft.

2 Roll out the mixture into a long "sausage" shape and cut it into 20 pieces.

3 Flatten and twist each piece and serve in *petits-fours* cases.

WHITE CHOCOLATE PUFFS

Makes 24

125g (5oz) white chocolate, melted
50g (2oz) puffed rice
25g (1oz) butter, melted
1tsp rum essence

1 Stir all the ingredients together and spoon into *petits-fours* cases.

2 Chill the sweets in the refrigerator until set.

WHISKY FUDGE CRACKERS

Makes 28 bars

FOR THE SWEETS:

100g (4oz) raisins
4tbsp whisky
225g (8oz) plain chocolate
225g (8oz) plain chocolate-
 flavoured cake covering
50g (2oz) caster sugar
397g (14.5oz) can condensed
 milk

TO FINISH:

Cellophane
Tartan ribbon

1 Soak the raisins in whisky overnight.

2 Put the chocolates in a pan with the sugar and heat gently until the sugar has dissolved. Stir in the condensed milk and raisins. Beat hard for 1 minute until the mixture starts to thicken. Spoon into an oiled 18 × 28 × 3.8cm (7 × 11 × 1½in) tin. Chill until firm.

3 Cut into 28, 2 × 9cm (¾ × 3½in) bars. Wrap in cellophane, twist the ends to seal, and tie with tartan ribbon.

CITRUS SURPRISES

Makes 2 packages

FOR THE MARZIPAN:

225g (8oz) ground almonds
225g (8oz) caster sugar
1tbsp liquid glucose
1 egg white
1tbsp grated orange rind
1tbsp grated lemon rind
Yellow food colouring
Orange food colouring
Whole cloves

FOR THE WRAPPING:

Orange crepe paper
Yellow crepe paper
Green crepe paper
1 grapefruit
1 lemon
Glue

1 Mix together the ground almonds, caster sugar, glucose and egg white. Knead to a smooth paste. Cut the mixture in half. Knead the orange rind and a little orange food colouring into one half, and the lemon rind and a few drops of yellow colouring into the other half.

2 Mould the orange marzipan into small orange shapes and the yellow marzipan into small lemon shapes. Roll the sides gently over a nutmeg grater to create a textured effect and insert whole cloves into the ends for stalks. Put the shapes into sweet cases and leave to dry overnight. Note: the cloves should be discarded before eating.

3 To wrap, bind a strip of orange crepe paper around the grapefruit. Glue the short ends of one side together. Make pleats in the paper at the remaining edges to achieve a rounded shape. Trim away the excess paper and glue at the base. Open the top carefully and remove the grapefruit, then fill the paper case with sweets. Glue the top pleats in place. Finally, cut the green paper into leaf shapes and glue in place. To make the lemon parcel, shape the yellow paper around a lemon, twist the ends to make points, then continue as for the grapefruit.

COCONUT NICE

Makes 8 bags

FOR THE COCONUT ICE:

3 egg whites
675g (1½lb) sifted icing sugar
250g (9oz) desiccated coconut
Water
Pink food colouring
Green food colouring

FOR THE GIFT BAGS:

Shiny wrapping paper
Stapler
Adhesive

1 Whisk the egg whites until frothy, then stir in the icing sugar and desiccated coconut. Mix to a stiff paste with 1-2tbsp water.

2 Divide the mixture into 3. With the food colouring, colour one third pink, one third green and leave one third plain white.

3 Press the green mixture evenly into the base of a lightly oiled 18 × 28 × 3.8cm (7 × 11 × 1½in) tin. Spread the white mixture over the top in an even layer, followed by the pink layer. Smooth the top and leave to dry at room temperature overnight. Cut into 60, 1 × 2.5cm (½ × 1in) bars.

4 To make the gift bags, cut a 28 × 10cm (11 × 4in) strip of wrapping paper. Mark the middle. Make small pleats to the right of the centre. When the pleated section measures 5cm (2in), staple the pleats along the bottom edge. Bring the short ends of the strip together and staple. Fold the base of the stapled pleats and glue to the back of the bag. Trim the tops of the pleats to points. For the handle, cut a 15 × 2cm (6 × ¾in) strip of paper, fold under the cut edges, glue. Glue both ends to the bag.

MOCHA CREAMS

Makes 1 box

FOR THE CHOCOLATES:

100g (4oz) plain chocolate
250ml (½pt) double cream
1tbsp sifted cocoa powder
1tbsp sifted icing sugar
1tbsp brandy
1tbsp instant coffee powder
12 foil sweet cases

FOR THE BOX:

A shallow box with a lid
Shiny patterned and plain gold
 wrapping paper
Glue
Fine giftwrap ribbon

1 Melt the plain chocolate in a bowl over a pan of simmering water. Brush the inside of 12 foil sweet cases thinly with chocolate, then chill until the chocolate has just set (about 15 minutes). Melt the unused chocolate again and add a second layer, then chill the cases until set.

2 Whip the double cream with the cocoa and icing sugar until just thick. Stir in the brandy and coffee powder. Spoon the mixture into a piping bag fitted with a medium star nozzle and pipe the mixture into the chocolate cases. Chill overnight.

3 For the box, cover a flat box with patterned paper. Line the base and sides with gold paper. Fill with chocolates and fasten with ribbon ties. Note: the chocolates can be stored in the refrigerator for up to a week.

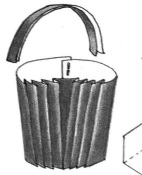

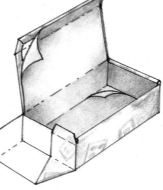

NUT FANDANGLES

Makes 7 strings

50g (2oz) blanched almonds
50g (2oz) hazelnuts
450g (1lb) granulated sugar
125ml (¼pt) water
1tbsp lemon juice

FOR THE WRAPPINGS:

Coloured cellophane
Narrow ribbon

1 Put the almonds and hazelnuts on a baking sheet and place under the grill until golden brown. Cool.

2 Put the sugar, water and lemon juice in a pan and heat gently, stirring occasionally, until the sugar has completely dissolved and the liquid is clear. Stop stirring, bring to the boil and continue cooking until the liquid reaches 160°C (325°F) on a sugar thermometer or until it resembles a light caramel colour. Remove the pan from the heat and gradually stir in the almonds and hazelnuts. Using a tablespoon, remove the nuts in clusters of three and put on oiled baking sheets to cool.

3 For the wrappings, cut out a long strip of coloured cellophane, 8cm (3½in) wide. Fold around each sweet cluster, twisting to enclose. Add the next sweet and twist again. Continue wrapping and twisting in this way until the chain is complete. Tie the ribbon along the chain and knot between each cluster at each twist. Finish with a bow.

TOFFEE APPLE APPEAL

Makes 8

FOR THE APPLES:

1.3m (4ft) thin wooden dowelling
8 dessert apples
150g (6oz) golden syrup
325g (12oz) demerara sugar
25g (1oz) butter
1tsp vinegar

FOR THE WRAPPINGS:

Cellophane
Ribbon

1 Cut the wooden dowelling into 15cm (6in) lengths.

2 Remove the stalks from the apples, wash and dry. Push the wooden dowelling "skewer" through the core of each apple.

3 Put the remaining ingredients into a large pan and heat gently without stirring until the sugar has dissolved. Boil to 143°C (290°F) or until a teaspoon of the mixture forms pliable strands when dropped into a saucer of cold water, drained and pulled apart with the fingers.

4 Remove the pan from the heat and quickly dip the apples into the toffee, twisting all the time so that they are coated evenly. Leave to cool and harden on an oiled baking sheet.

5 When cold, wrap in cellophane and tie with ribbon.

CHOCOLATE TRUFFLE TREE

Makes 3 boxes

FOR THE TRUFFLES:

150g (6oz) plain chocolate

100g (4oz) plain chocolate-flavoured cake covering

3tbsp double cream

1tbsp rum

2tbsp icing sugar

2tbsp cocoa powder

FOR THE TREE:

Cardboard

Shiny green wrapping paper

20.5 × 20.5cm (8 × 8in) stiff acetate (available from art shops)

Crayon

Green sticky stars

Glue

Gold cord

1 Melt the chocolates in a bowl over a pan of simmering water. Cool. Put the cream in a small pan and heat until just boiling. Cool. Add the cream to the chocolate with the rum. Chill for about 45 minutes or until firm. Sift the icing sugar and the cocoa onto separate plates. Roll a teaspoonful of the truffle mixture in either the icing sugar or the cocoa, then put the coated truffle balls into individual foil cases.

2 To make the tree, draw one complete tree shape in cardboard, using the diagram (below) for reference. Cut out. To make the sides of the box, cut out long strips of card measuring 3.8cm (1½in) in width, fold in 1cm (½in) along one long edge of each strip and glue this onto the tree base. Cover the entire box with shiny paper. For the lid, use a crayon to draw a tree shape on acetate to the same dimensions as your box. Cut out, allowing an extra 2.5cm (1in) all around. Fold along the crayon lines, then stick the stars on top. Fill the box with chocolates. Tuck the lid into the box and tie with cord.

CHERRY CHOCOLATES

Makes 1 box

225g (8oz) white almond paste

20 maraschino cherries

150g (6oz) plain chocolate

150g (6oz) white chocolate

Desiccated coconut or chocolate strands

Icing sugar for dusting

1 Knead the almond paste until soft and divide into 20 even pieces. Next, roll out each piece to a circle the size of a large coin on a surface dusted with icing sugar.

2 Dry the maraschino cherries on kitchen paper and wrap each one in a circle of almond paste.

3 Melt the plain and white chocolate separately in individual bowls set over pans of simmering water. Dip half of the almond-covered cherries into white chocolate and half into plain chocolate. Decorate by drizzling over a contrasting chocolate or sprinkling with desiccated coconut or chocolate strands. Leave them to set, then dust each chocolate with icing sugar. Put the chocolate-coated cherries into 20 *petits-fours* cases.

4 Place in a decorated box to serve.

CHEESE BISCUITS

Makes 675g (1½lb)
450g (1lb) plain flour
1tsp salt
2tsp dried mustard
250g (9oz) margarine
225g (8oz) grated Cheddar
  cheese
1 egg, beaten
Water
Egg for glazing
Poppy or sesame seeds

1 Sieve the flour with the salt and dried mustard, then rub in the margarine. Add the cheese and egg, together with enough water to make a firm dough.

2 Roll out, stamp out shapes with small cutters and put onto baking sheets. Glaze with egg and then sprinkle with poppy seeds or sesame seeds.

3 Bake at 200°C (400°F/Gas 6) for 8-10 minutes, then place on a wire rack to cool.

BAGS OF FLAVOUR

TO MAKE EACH BOUQUET GARNI:
Muslin
Thread or ribbon
½tsp ground marjoram
½tsp dried basil
½tsp dried oregano
½tsp dried thyme
2 bay leaves

1 Fold the muslin in half and cut out a double-thickness circle about 7.5cm (3in) in diameter. Place the mixed herbs inside and secure with thread or ribbon.

TO MAKE EACH MULLED-WINE SACHET:
Muslin
Thread or ribbon
½ broken cinammon stick
Small piece of dried root ginger
8 whole cloves
Strips of orange zest

1 Fold the muslin in half and cut out a circle as above. Fill with the spices and the orange zest, and secure with thread or ribbon.

BOMBAY PASTA SHELLS

Serves 8
150g (6oz) dried pasta shells
1tbsp vegetable oil
2tbsp plain flour
Oil for deep frying
2tsp chilli powder
2tsp ground cumin
2tsp ground coriander
½tsp sugar
¼ tsp salt
TO FINISH:
Cellophane
Ribbon

1 Cook the pasta in salted water with 1tbsp oil for about 10 minutes or until *"al dente"*. Drain, rinse with cold water and drain again. Toss in flour.

2 Half fill a saucepan or deep-fat fryer with oil and heat to 180°C (350°F) on a thermometer or until a cube of bread, when dropped in the oil, rises to the surface. Cook the pasta, a handful at a time, for 4-5 minutes or until golden brown. Drain on kitchen paper.

3 Mix together the chilli powder, cumin, coriander, sugar and salt. Sprinkle over the pasta and leave to cool. Divide the pasta into 8 portions. Wrap in cellophane and tie with ribbon.

MUESLI

Makes 1.4kg (3lb)
250g (9oz) dried fruit salad
1kg (2¼lb) muesli mix
4tbsp sunflower seeds
100g (4oz) chopped hazelnuts
100g (4oz) sultanas

1 Mix all the ingredients together in a large bowl. Pour into a large, labelled storage jar and tie with ribbon.

MINI RUMTOPFS

Makes 3 jars

900g (2lb) satsumas
225g (8oz) seedless black grapes
225g (8oz) seedless white grapes
900g (2lb) fresh pineapple
900g (2lb) caster sugar
375ml (¾pt) rum

TO FINISH:

Wrapping paper
Ribbon
3 200g (7oz) coffee jars

1 Peel the satsumas and remove the pith. Wash and dry the grapes. Cut off the base of the pineapple so that it stands up, then, using a knife, cut off the skin in downward strips. Cut the flesh into small pieces. Place the fruits into separate bowls and sprinkle with sugar. Stand for 2 hours.

2 Layer the black grapes and juices in the jars and cover with rum. Repeat with the remaining fruit, covering each layer with rum.

3 Cover with plastic kitchen film and lids, then decorate with wrapping paper and ribbon.

DRESSING UP

Each makes 625ml (1¼pt)

WALNUT VINAIGRETTE:

500ml (1pt) sunflower oil
125ml (¼pt) white-wine vinegar
Salt and pepper
3 walnut halves

1 Combine the oil with the wine vinegar and seasoning. Divide between bottles, add the walnut halves. Seal.

TARRAGON VINAIGRETTE:

500ml (1pt) sunflower oil
125ml (¼pt) tarragon vinegar
Salt and pepper
Fresh tarragon

1 Mix the oil with the vinegar and seasoning. Bottle, add a sprig of fresh tarragon to each bottle and seal.

HOT AND SPICY:

500ml (1pt) sunflower oil
125ml (¼pt) red-wine vinegar

1tsp Tabasco
½tsp crushed black pepper

1 Combine the ingredients, bottle and seal.

FRENCH DRESSING:

375ml (¾pt) sunflower oil
125ml (¼pt) olive oil
125ml (¼pt) white-wine vinegar
1tsp coarse grain mustard
Salt and pepper.

1 Combine the ingredients, bottle, seal. Shake well before serving.

great GIFTS

SOMETHING TO RELISH

Makes 4.5kg (10lb)

1.2kg (2½lb) courgettes
2 large red peppers
2tbsp salt
2tbsp flour
1tbsp turmeric
3tbsp dried mustard powder
3tbsp ground ginger
1.1 litre (2pt) distilled malt vinegar
150g (6oz) sugar
1.4kg (3lb) frozen sweetcorn

1 Trim and thinly slice the courgettes. Chop the peppers, mix with the courgettes and salt, cover and leave overnight.

2 Rinse the vegetables and put into a large pan. Combine the flour with the turmeric, mustard, flour and ginger and mix to a smooth paste with the vinegar. Add to the pan, together with the sugar. Bring to the boil, stirring all the time. Add the sweetcorn and bring to the boil. Simmer for 10 minutes. Pour into jars, cool and seal.

2

PRESENT PERFECT

WHETHER YOU'RE HANDY WITH A NEEDLE OR JUST A BEGIN-
NER, IT'S EAST TO TURN LEFT-OVER FABRICS INTO FUN TOYS
AND ACCESSORIES. DELVE INTO THE REMNANT BOX AND
TURN YOUR SCRAPS OF MATERIAL INTO TREASURE! EVEN THE
SMALLEST REMNANTS CAN BE PRESSED INTO USE TO MAKE
PRETTY GIFTS FOR CHRISTMAS FAIRS OR SCHOOL FUND-
RAISERS. WE'VE COME UP WITH SOME NOVEL VARIATIONS
ON TRADITIONAL GIFTS – TRY OUR DESIGN FOR BEANBAG
DINOSAURS – PLUS A SELECTION OF TRIED AND TRUSTED
KNITTED FAVOURITES. WHEN YOU'VE FINISHED YOUR
LABOURS, ADD A PERSONAL TOUCH WITH OUR CROSS-STITCH
GIFT TAGS. THEY'RE QUICK TO SEW AND WILL ADD A STYLISH
TOUCH TO EVEN THE HUMBLEST GIFT.

SANTA'S SACK

1 pillow
Felt squares in assorted colours
Tracing paper
1m (39in) thick cord
Fabric glue
FOR THE SNOWMAN:
35 × 25cm (13¾ × 9¾in) white
    fleece
plus 35 × 25cm (13¾ × 9¾in)
    double-sided iron-on adhesive
    webbing
FOR THE TREE:
40.5 × 35cm (16 × 13¾in)
    green fabric
plus 40 × 35cm (16 × 13¾in)
    double-sided iron-on adhesive
    webbing

1 Using the pattern (right) for reference, draw up a pattern for the snowman or tree to the correct size onto tracing paper. 1 square = 4cm (1½in).

2 Iron the adhesive webbing onto the white fleece or green fabric following the manufacturer's instructions, then pin the paper pattern onto the fabric and cut out the shape.

3 Following the manufacturer's instructions, apply the snowman or tree to the pillowcase.

4 Using the main picture for reference, trace off the templates from p.60 and cut out the snowman's details or tree decorations in felt. Stick them on using fabric glue. If you are making the tree, decorate the parcels with scraps of ribbon.

5 Finally, tie up the top of the sack using a length of cord.

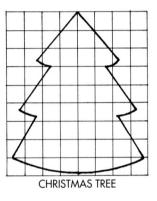

SNOWMAN

CHRISTMAS TREE

CROSS-STITCH CARDS

7 × 7cm (2¾ × 2¾in) Aida
    evenweave
33 × 16cm (13 × 6in) red or
    green cardboard
Green and red embroidery
    thread
Embroidery needle
Craft knife
Adhesive tape
Double-sided adhesive tape

1 Using cross stitch, embroider the Christmas tree, following the chart (shown opposite).

2 Next, fold the cardboard into three and using a craft knife cut out a square window from the central panel measuring 5 × 5cm (2 × 2in).

3 Place the embroidered square behind the window and tape it to the card. Finally stick the inner flap in place behind the front flap and secure it with double-sided adhesive tape.

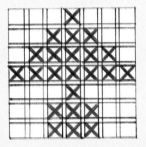

SANTA'S STOCKING
Materials

1 × 50g ball Double Knitting in Main Colour (M); ½ ball in Contrast (C); scraps in various colours for Swiss darning; pair 4mm (No.8) knitting needles

Measurements: length of foot 33cm (13in); length of leg 51cm (20in)

Tension: 22 sts and 30 rows to 10cm (4in) over st-st on 4mm needles

Abbreviations: alt – alternate; **beg** – beginning; **cm** – centimetres; **cont** – continue; **dec** – decrease; **foll** – following; **g-st** – garter stitch; **in** – inches; **inc** – increase; **K** – knit; **P** – purl; **rep** – repeat; **RS** – right side; **st(s)** – stitch(es); **st-st** – stocking stitch; **tog** – together

1st side of foot: with M, cast on 50 sts. Work 6 rows in st-st, inc 1 st at each end of every row. (62 sts.) Inc 1 st at each end of next 5 alt rows. (72 sts.) Cont straight until work measures 10cm (4in) from cast-on edge, ending with a P row*.
**Shape toe:

next row: work to last 2 sts, work 2 tog. Work 1 row. Rep last 2 rows 4 times. (67 sts.) **Next row:** work to last 2 sts, work 2 tog. **Next row:** work 2 tog, work to end. Rep last 2 rows twice, then work the first of the 2 rows again. (60 sts.) Cast off 15 sts at beg of next row. Dec 1 st at end of next row and at same edge on foll 4 rows, thus ending with a K row. (40 sts) ******. Cut off yarn and leave sts on a spare needle.

2nd side of foot: work as 1st side to * but work 1 less row, thus ending with a K row. Work as 1st side of foot from ** to ** but note that final row will be a P row. Do not cut off yarn. K 1 row.

Leg: P across 40 sts of 2nd side of foot then P across 40 sts of 1st side of foot. (80 sts.) Cont straight until work measures 46cm (18in) from cast-on edge, ending with a P row. Change to C and work 10cm (4in) in g-st. Cast off.

To complete: Swiss darn name centrally down leg, spacing letters 4 rows apart – longer names may have to be abbreviated. Swiss darn holly, tree and parcels as desired, noting that chart for holly may be used vertically or horizontally. Join leg and foot seams. Fold g-st section in half onto RS.

SWISS DARNING

This is a way of embroidering over stocking stitch using a needle and yarn of similar thickness to the background. The finished effect is as if it had been knitted in. Starting at the base of the first stitch to be covered, bring the needle through from back to front. Insert the needle from right to left at the base of the stitch above, then insert it back into the base of the first stitch, coming out at the base of the next stitch to be covered.

ROLL UP! ROLL UP!

1 sheet each of black and white cartridge paper
Craft knife
PVA adhesive
2 ¼ mm (No. 13) knitting needle
Ruler
Paintbrush
Nylon thread
Bodkin

1 Using a craft knife, cut both sheets of cartridge paper into long triangles as follows. Large beads: triangle base 5cm (2in), length 53.5cm (21in); medium round beads: base 2cm (1in), length 53.5cm (21in); long thin beads: base 1cm (½in), length 10cm (4in).

2 Brush adhesive over one side of the paper triangle to within 2cm (¾in) of the base. Starting at the base, roll the paper triangle tightly around the knitting needle.

3 Coat the outside of the paper bead with adhesive then carefully remove the bead from the knitting needle and leave it to dry.

4 To make the necklace or bracelet, thread an assortment of beads onto a piece of nylon thread and secure the ends with a firm knot. You could also make earrings in the same way: simply use a bodkin to pierce a hole in the top of one of the paper beads and attach it to a triangle wire and earring wire.

fashion
FUN

SMART SLIDES

1 hair slide
30cm (12in) gold dressing-gown braid
Thread
15cm (6in) strung pearls
Glue

1 Bind the ends of the braid together with thread, then fold in half to produce four thicknesses. Starting at one end, twist the lengths tightly together, binding in the pearls as you twist. Finally, fix the braid to the slide with glue.

HAIR TWIST

70 × 9cm (27½ × 3½in) fabric
16cm (6½in) narrow elastic

1 Fold the fabric in half with right sides together and long edges matching. Join the long edges taking a 5mm (¼in) seam and leaving 2.5cm (1in) unsewn at each end. Turn through.

2 Join the short ends with right sides together to form a ring.

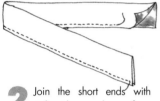

3 Thread elastic through the ring and stitch the ends together firmly. Turn in and stitch the raw edges at the opening.

HAIRBAND

70 × 9cm (27½ × 3½in) fabric
Plain plastic hairband
Fabric adhesive

1 Fold the fabric in half with right sides together and long edges matching, then stitch the long edges together. Turn through.

2 Slip the fabric tube onto the hairband. Spread adhesive over the ends of the hairband, on the underside.

3 Stick the ends of the fabric to the hairband, making sure that you first turn in the raw edges, and slipstitch neatly at the back to fit tightly.

KNOTTY BUT NICE

1m (39in) narrow cord in two colours
Key ring

1 Treating the two cords as one, pass them through the key ring and tie a Chinese button knot (see diagrams).

2 Tie a few half hitches to form the central column.

3 Finish with another Chinese button knot and fringe the ends of the cord. Trim to about 3cm (1¼in). As an alternative, omit the first Chinese button knot.

DESIGNER T-SHIRTS

Plain white T-shirt
Fabric pens in assorted colours
Cardboard

1 First, wash, dry and press the T-shirt, then place a piece of cardboard inside the garment to prevent the paint from seeping through to the back. If you don't want to draw freehand on the garment, draw your design onto the cardboard before you place it inside the T-shirt and trace your design through to the front. Make sure that you position the cardboard carefully before applying the colour to the fabric.

2 Using fabric pens, draw your design on the T-shirt. Leave to dry, then press with a hot iron over a dry cloth to fix the colours.

POTPOURRI CUSHION

60 × 90cm (23½ × 35½in) cotton lawn

15 × 15cm (6 × 6in) butter muslin

80cm (31½in) narrow ribbon

Wadding

Two handfuls of potpourri

1 From the cotton lawn, cut two 31 × 31cm (12¼ × 12¼in) squares and three lengths measuring 5 × 90cm (2 × 35½in). Position the muslin in the middle of one cotton lawn square. Stitch the muslin to the cotton lawn along three sides and stuff with potpourri. Finally, stitch the fourth side.

2 For the frill, join the three lengths of cotton lawn together along their short edges. Next, with wrong sides together press the strip in half lengthways. Make running stitches along the double-thickness raw edges, then gather and tack the frill around the muslin square.

3 Cut out a co-ordinating strip of fabric measuring 3.2 × 63.5cm (1¼ × 25in). Turn in 3mm (⅛in) along the raw edges and use this to cover the raw edges of the frill.

4 Cut the ribbon into four equal lengths, then stitch to the corners of the frill.

5 To make up the cushion, pin the front cotton lawn square to the back cotton lawn square with right sides together. Stitch the cushion squares together along three sides and turn to the right side. Finally, stuff with wadding and slipstitch the opening.

> **All seam allowances are 1cm (⅜in) unless otherwise stated. To draw templates, use a soft pencil and tracing paper.**

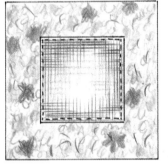

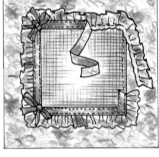

FAST FRAMES

Stiff cardboard

Wrapping paper

Photograph

Adhesive tape

Glue

Ruler

Craft knife

1 Using a craft knife, cut two pieces of cardboard to the same size. Cut a window in the middle of one shape to suit the size of your photograph. Cover one side of each piece of cardboard with wrapping paper, making sure that you leave the window area free from paper.

2 Position the photograph behind the window and secure it to the reverse of the cardboard with adhesive tape. Glue the frame front to the frame back and leave to dry.

3 To make the stand, cut a 12 × 2.5cm (4¾ × 1in) strip of cardboard. Cover this with wrapping paper. Score across the width 3.2cm (1¼in) from one end, then stick to the frame back.

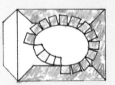

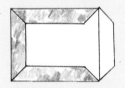

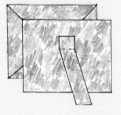

SPICY POMANDERS

Oranges
Cloves
Ribbon
Felt pen
Fork

1 Divide the orange into quarters using your felt pen. Pierce the peel evenly all over with a fork, making sure that you leave four narrow strips of rind free from holes for the ribbon.

2 Push a clove into each hole, then leave the pomander to dry in a warm, dark place for at least two weeks.

3 To finish, tie ribbon around the pomander, parcel fashion.

pretty
AND PERFUMED

POTPOURRI SACHETS

Scraps of lace
60 × 2cm (23½ × ¾in) lace edging per sachet
A handful of potpourri
Silk flowers
Beads
Paper

1 Draw a circle or oval shape 10cm (4in) in diameter onto paper. Use this as a template to cut two shapes from lace for each sachet.

2 Sew running stitches along the lace edging, gather and tack this around the circumference of one circle. With right sides together and raw edges even, place the remaining circle on top of the lace circle and stitch (A), leaving a gap for turning. Turn through.

3 Fill the sachet with potpourri and slipstitch the opening.

4 Finally, stitch on the flowers and beads (B).

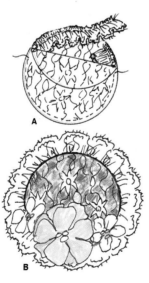

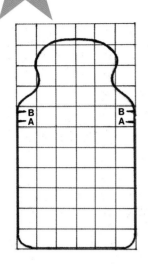
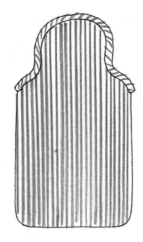
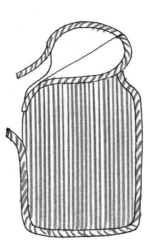

COSY TOES

50cm (19½ in) of 90cm (35½ in) wide quilted fabric, plus scraps of toning fabric *or* 50cm (19½ in) of 90cm (35½ in) wide striped fabric

60 × 50cm (23½ × 19½ in) each of thin wadding and plain lining

30cm (12in) ribbon

Touch-and-close tape *or* snap fasteners

Metric graph paper

To quilt your own fabric, place the fabric and the lining right sides out, sandwiching the wadding between them. Tack the three layers together, then quilt parallel lines of stitching spaced 3.5cm (1⅜ in) apart.

1 Draw a pattern to the correct size (1sq = 4cm/1⅝ in) and use this to cut out two pieces from quilted fabric. From the fabric scraps, cut enough 3.5cm (1⅜ in) wide bias strips to make a continuous 1.5m (5ft) length. Use this strip to bind the top edge of one quilted piece between points A.

2 Machine quilt the pieces together around the side and lower edges between points B, stitching close to the edge. Bind the raw edges, making sure that you hold the finished top edge clear while you bind the remaining one.

3 Stitch the centre of the ribbon to the centre back of the neck and tie in a bow at the front. Stitch touch-and-close tape or snap fasteners to the inside neck to fasten securely.

time
FOR BED

A COUPLE OF CUTIES

FOR THE DOLL:
20 × 90cm (7¾ × 35½in) pink fabric
Scrap of blue fabric
20 × 115cm (7¾ × 45¼in) floral fabric

FOR THE TEDDY:
20 × 115cm (7¾ × 45¼in) pink towelling
Black embroidery cotton
Scrap of thin ribbon

FOR BOTH:
Scraps of felt
Bag of toy filling
400g (1lb) split peas
Fabric glue

1 Using the templates from p.56, trace off and cut out the fabric as follows. For the doll, you will need to cut two arms, two legs and two heads from pink fabric, together with two bodies from blue fabric and two pieces of felt for the hair. For the teddy, you will need two arms, two legs, two heads and two bodies from pink towelling, then four ears and a nose from felt.

2 Stitch the seams on each limb (A and B). Turn through, stuff with toy filling and slipstitch the openings. With right sides together, stitch the teddy's ears together in pairs, then turn

both sets through to the right side.

3 Stitch each head to a body piece, making sure that for the teddy you include the ears in the seamline of the head. Tack the limbs in position on the body (C), then stitch the front to the back, leaving a gap in side D. Turn through. Stuff the head with toy filling and slipstitch the neck along the seams through all layers.

4 Fill the body with split peas and slipstitch the gap.

5 Cut out and stick on the doll and teddy features. Stitch the doll's front and back hair together and stick to the head (E). Embroider the teddy's mouth (F) and tie a ribbon around his neck.

6 For the skirt, cut out a main piece of floral fabric measuring 10 × 115cm (4 × 45¼in) and a waistband measuring 23 × 3.2cm (9 × 1¼in). Join the short edges of the main piece together to form a circle. Hem along one edge and gather the remaining edge. On the waistband, turn and press both the long edges to the centre, then press the band in half lengthways. Sandwich the gathered skirt edge between the folded band and stitch (G). Cut out and stitch felt bows to the skirt. Finally, secure the skirt to the body with a few stitches.

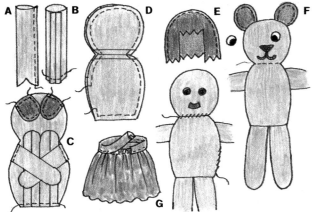

FRIENDLY FELLOWS

50 × 30cm (19½ × 12in) fabric
Wadding
Felt scraps
Tracing paper
Buttons

1 Fold the tracing paper in half and place the fold along the dotted line of the template on

p.56. Trace off the outline and cut out the shape. Open out. Fold the fabric in half with right sides together and draw around the template onto the fabric. Cut out the shapes (you should have two in all).

2 With right sides together and raw edges even, stitch around the outline, leaving a gap between the notches. Cut out, leaving 6-mm (¼in) turnings. Clip the curved edges. Turn through, stuff and slipstitch the opening neatly.

3 Finally, cut out and stitch on the felt features, buttons and bow tie.

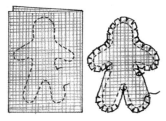

fun
FACTORY

BEST-DRESSED FROGS

Corduroy fabric
450g (1lb) split peas
Tracing paper
Scrap of lace and scrap of velvet ribbon *or* string of beads
2 buttons

1 Trace off the frog template from p.57 onto tracing paper and place this on the fabric. Cut out two shapes. With right sides together and raw edges even, stitch the two pieces together, leaving a gap between the legs for turning. Turn through.

2 Fill the bag with split peas and slipstitch the opening.

3 Stitch on the buttons for the eyes. For Mrs Frog, stitch a bead necklace and bracelet in place, while for Mr Frog, attach a lace shirt front and tie a piece of velvet ribbon around his neck.

BEANBAG MICE

Felt scraps
225g (8oz) split peas
Embroidery thread
Adhesive
Needle and thread

1 Trace off the templates on p.57 and cut out two bodies, one mouse base and two ears from felt.

2 With wrong sides together and raw edges even, stitch the body pieces together, leaving the base open. Next, stitch the base to the body, leaving a gap for the stuffing. Fill with split peas and slipstitch the opening.

3 Cut out and stick on two felt eyes, then stitch on the ears and attach embroidery thread for the whiskers.

4 To make the tail, plait together lengths of embroidery thread and stitch them to the rear end.

FINGER FRIENDS

FOR EACH LARGE BIRD:
2 pieces of felt, measuring 12 × 10cm (4¾ × 4in)
FOR EACH SMALL BIRD:
2 pieces of felt, measuring 7 × 5cm (2¾ × 2in)
Wadding scraps *or* lavender
Contrasting felt for the face, eyes and beak
Fabric adhesive
Embroidery thread and needle

1 Trace off the template on p.57 to make a pattern, then cut out two pieces of felt for each bird. For the large bird, fold the felt in half lengthways and use the template up to the fold line only. Cut out the pieces for the face, beak and eyes from a contrasting coloured felt, making sure that you adjust the shape of the features for the different bird types. Stick these to the front of each bird using fabric glue.

3 Embroider the pupils. Oversew the sides and stuff the larger birds with wadding or lavender. Stitch on a felt oval to form the base.

BRONTOSAURUS BEANBAGS

30.5 × 90cm (12 × 35½in)
fabric
Contrasting felt square
Scraps of black and white felt
225g (8oz) split peas or lentils
Tracing paper

1 Trace off the templates from p.58, putting the folded paper to the dotted line for the underbody. From the fabric, cut one underbody and two top pieces (for the beanbag – C – cut two heads and two body tops). From the felt, cut the fin, neck frill or spots.

2 For bag A, join the top pieces with a 6mm (¼in) seam. For bag B, join the top pieces as before enclosing the dorsal fin. For bag C, join the head pieces along the straight edges and top body pieces then join the head to the body, making sure that you enclose the neck frill.

3 With right sides together and raw edges even, stitch the top to the underbody, taking a 6mm (¼in) seam and leaving a gap for turning. Clip curves and turn through to right side. Fill with split peas and stitch the opening. Glue on the eyes and the spots.

FOLLOW MY LEADER

Felt squares in two colours
Toy stuffing
Felt scraps in black and white
Tracing paper
Adhesive
Our template on p.57 makes the middle-sized elephant. Use a photocopier to enlarge or decrease the pattern for the other sizes.

1 Trace off the template from p.57 and cut out two bodies and two undersides from felt. From the contrasting colour, cut out two ears and one tail.

2 With right sides together and raw edges even, stitch together the underbody pieces along the long curved edge. Next, with wrong sides together, stitch the underbody to the bodies around the leg edges. Stitch around the rest of the body, leaving a gap for stuffing. Fill with toy stuffing, then stitch across the opening.

3 Sew on the ears and tail. Finally, cut out and stick on the felt eyes.

BAKERS' BUTTONS

Synthetic modelling clay in red and black
Tiny canapé or aspic cutters
Bodkin
Coloured cardboard for mounting

1 To make the star buttons, roll out the black modelling clay to a thickness of 3mm (⅛in), and, using the cutters, cut out six shapes. Lay them on a baking tray and pierce two holes in each star with a bodkin.

2 To make the oval buttons, roll out the red modelling clay to a thickness of 3mm (⅛in). Using the diagram for reference, cut out six oval shapes and lay them on a baking tray. Pierce two holes in each oval button with a bodkin.

3 Following the manufacturer's instructions, bake the shapes in an oven for the recommended time. Finally, sew the buttons onto cardboard for presentation.

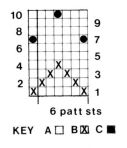

Materials

Hayfield Grampian DK (45% acrylic/40% Bri-Nylon/15% wool) in 50g balls: 2 balls Scarlet (A), 1 ball each Navy (B) and Daffodil (C); pair each 3¼mm (No.10) and 4mm (No.8) knitting needles; set of four 4mm (No.8) double-pointed needles.

Measurements

BERET: to fit average adults.
MITTS: length 23cm (9in); all round measurement above thumb 19.5cm (7¾in).
Tension: 22 sts and 25 rows to 10cm (4in) over patt on 4mm needles.

6 patt sts

KEY A □ B ☒ C ■

BERET

With 3¼mm needles and A, cast on 125 sts.
1st rib row (RS): K 1, [P 1, K 1] to end. **2nd rib row:** P 1, [K 1, P 1] to end. Rep these 2 rows twice, then work 1st rib row again. **Inc row:** rib 3, [inc in next st, rib 5, inc in next st, rib 6] 9 times, inc in next st, rib 4. (144 sts.) Change to 4mm needles. Cont in st-st. Work 4 rows. **Inc row:** [K 1, M 1, K 22, M 1, K 1] 6 times. Beg with a P row, st-st 5 rows. **Inc rows:** [K 1, M 1, K 24, M 1, K 1] 6 times. Beg with a P row, st-st 5 rows. **Inc row:** [K 1, M 1, K 26, M 1, K 1] 6 times. (180 sts.) Beg with a P row, st-st 3 rows. Work 10 rows of chart, reading odd-numbered K rows from right to left and even-numbered P rows from left to right; rep 6 patt sts 30 times on every row. **Shape work:** now cont in patt as 5th to 10th rows of chart, taking care to keep patt correct and noting that each dec should be worked with A. **Dec row:** [K 1, K 2 tog, K 24, skpo, K 1] 6 times. Work 1 row. **Dec row:** [K 1, K 2 tog, K 22, skpo, K 1] 6 times. Work 1 row. **Dec row:** [K 1, K 2 tog, K 20, skpo, K 1] 6 times. Cont to dec in this way on every RS row, working 2 sts less between pair of decs on each successive row, until 12 sts rem, ending with a WS row. Break off yarn, thread end through rem sts, draw up and secure. Join seam. Make a small pompon with B and sew to top.

RIGHT MITT

With 3¼mm needles and A, cast on 37 sts. Rib 5cm as at beg of beret, ending with a 2nd rib row.

Change to 4mm needles. Cont in st-st. Work 2 rows. **Inc row:** K 18, [K into front and back of next st] 6 times, K 13. (43 sts.) P 1 row. Cont from chart: **1st row (RS):** reading 1st row from right to left, K 6 patt sts 7 times, K last st of chart. **2nd row:** reading 2nd row from left to right, P 1st st of chart, P 6 patt sts 7 times. Patt 3rd to 10th rows, then work 5th to 8th rows again. **Thumb opening row:** K 21, sl next 6 sts onto a safety pin for thumb, cast on 6 sts, K 16. (43 sts.) Patt 10th row of chart. Rep 5th to 10th rows of chart until work measures 20cm (7¾in) from beg, ending with a WS row. **Top shaping: 1st row:** keeping patt correct, K 1, [skpo, patt 16, K 2 tog, K 1] twice. Patt 1 row. **3rd row:** K 1, [skpo, patt 14, K 2 tog, K 1] twice. Patt 1 row. **5th row:** K 1, [skpo, patt 12, K 2 tog, K 1] twice. **6th row:** P 1, [P 2 tog, patt 10, P 2 tog TBL, P 1] twice. **7th row:** K 1, [skpo, patt 8, K 2 tog, K 1], twice. Cast off rem 23 sts. **Thumb:** with RS facing and set of 4mm double-pointed needles, patt across 6 sts on safety pin then pick up and K 6 sts across 6 cast-on sts. (12 sts.) Keeping patt correct, cont in rounds for 5cm. **Dec round:** [K 2 tog] to end. Break off yarn, thread end through rem 6 sts, draw up and secure. Join top and side seam.

LEFT MITT

Make up the left mitt to match the right mitt, reversing the position of the thumb by working the inc row and the thumb opening row in reverse.

Abbreviations: beg – beginning); **cm** – centimetres; **ch** – chain; **cont** – continue; **dec** – decrease; **DC** – double crochet; **in** – inches; **inc** – increase; **K** – knit; **M1** – make 1 st by picking up a strand between needles and K it through back of loop; **P** – purl; **patt** – pattern; **rem** – remain(ing); **rep** – repeat; **RS** – right side; **sl** – slip; **skpo** – slip 1 st, knit 1 st, pass slipped st over; **st(s)** – stitch(es); **st-st** – stocking stitch; **TBL** – through back of loops; **tog** – together; **WS** – wrong side. Work instructions in square brackets the number of times given.

heart WARMERS

Materials

Hayfields Grampian DK (45% acrylic, 40% Bri-Nylon/15% wool) in 50g balls: 2 balls Navy (A) and 1 ball White (B); pair 4mm (No.8) needles.

Measurements

HAT: to fit average adults.

MITTS: length 24cm (9½in); all round measurement above thumb 18cm (7in).

Tension: 22 sts and 28 rows to 10cm (4in) over st-st on 4mm needles.

Abbreviations: see opposite.

HAT

With 4mm needles and A, cast on 129 sts. **1st rib row (RS):** K 1, [P 1, K 1] to end. **2nd rib row:** P 1 [K 1, P 1] to end. Rep these 2 rows for 8cm (3in), ending with a 2nd rib row. Cont in st-st from chart stranding colour not in use loosely across WS. **1st row (RS):** reading chart from right to left K 16 patt sts 8 times, K last st of chart. **2nd row:** reading chart from left to right, P 1st st of chart, P 16 patt sts 8 times. Beg with 3rd row, cont from chart until all 21 rows have been completed. Cont in A. **Dec row (WS):** P 4, [P 2 tog, P 5] to last 6 sts, P 2 tog, P 4. (111 sts.) Beg with a K row, cont in st-st until work measures 22cm (8½in) from cast-on edge, ending with a P row. **Top shaping: 1st row:** K 1, [K 2 tog, K 9] to end. **2nd and every WS row:** P. **3rd row:** K 1, [K 2 tog, K 8] to end. **5th row:** K 1, [K 2 tog, K 7] to end. Cont to dec in this way until 21 sts rem, end-

ing with a P row. **Next row:** K 1, [K 2 tog] to end. Break off yarn, thread end through rem 11 sts, draw up and secure. Taking ½ st from each edge into seam, join centre-back seam, reversing seam on lower 5cm (2in) of rib for brim.

RIGHT MITT

With 4mm needles and A, cast on 33 sts. Rib 8cm as hat, ending with a 2nd rib row and inc 6 sts evenly across. (39 sts.) Beg with a K row, st-st 2 rows. Work motif from chart: **1st row (RS):** K 1 A, reading chart from right to left K 16 patt sts, K last st of chart, K 21 A. **2nd row:** P 21 A, reading chart from left to right, P 1st st of chart, P 16 patt sts, P 1 A. Cont from chart shaping thumb thus: **3rd row:** K 1 A, patt 17, with A, K 1, M 1, K 1, M 1, K 19. **4th row:** P 23 A, patt 17, P 1 A. **5th row:** K 1 A, patt 17, with A, K 1, M 1, K 3, M 1, K 19. **6th row:** P 25 A, patt 17, P 1 A. **7th row:** K 1 A, patt 17, with A, K 1, M 1, K 5, M 1, K 19. **8th row:** P 27 A, patt 17, with A, P 1 A. **9th row:** K 1 A, patt 17, K 27 A. **10th row:** as 8th. **11th row:** K 1 A, patt 17, with A, K 1, M 1, K 7, M 1, K 19. 47 sts. **12th row:** P 29 A, patt 17, P 1 A. **13th row:** K 1 A, patt 17, K 29 A. **14th row:** as 12th. **15th row:** K 1 A, patt 17, K 10 A, turn. **Next row:** with A, cast on 1 st, P cast-on st, P 9 A, turn and cast on 1 st. Cont in A on these 11 sts only. St-st 10 rows. **Dec row:** K 1, [K 2 tog] to end. Break off yarn, thread end through rem 6 sts, draw up and secure. Join seam. **Next row:** with RS facing, rejoin A to inner end of sts on right needle, pick up and K 2 sts from base of thumb, K across 19 sts on left needle. (40 sts.) Beg with a P row, com-

plete chart then cont in A until work measures 20cm (7¾in) from cast-on edge, ending with a P row. **Top shaping: 1st row:** K 1, [K 2 tog TBL, K 15, K 2 tog] twice, K 1. P 1 row. **3rd row:** K 1, [K 2 tog TBL, K 13, K 2 tog] twice, K 1. P 1 row. **5th row:** K 1, [K 2 tog TBL, K 11, K 2 tog] twice, K 1. P 1 row. Cont to dec

in this way until 20 sts rem, ending with a P row. Cast off. Join seams.

LEFT MITT

Work to match right mitt, reversing position of motif thus: **1st row (RS):** K 21 A, reading chart from right to left K 16 patt sts, K last st of chart, K 1 A.

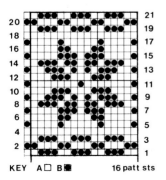

KEY   A □   B ■   16 patt sts

ANTLER ANTICS

Materials
Wendy Family Choice DK: Sweater: 2 (3) 50g balls M (Valentine); 1 ball each A (Purity), B (Video Jade) and C Bulrush). Hat: 1, 50g ball A; oddment of M for pompon; pair each 3¼mm (No.10) and 4mm (No.8) needles.

Measurements
To fit chest 56 (61)cm, 22 (24)in; actual measurement 59 (64)cm, 23¼ (25¼)in; length 30 (34)cm, 11¾ (13½)in; approximate sleeve length 26 (29)cm, 10¼ (11½)in. Figures in round brackets are for larger size.

Tension: 24 sts and 30 rows to 10cm (4in) over snowflake patt from chart 3 on 4mm needles.

Abbreviations: alt – alternate; **beg** – beginning; **cm** – centimetres; **cont** – continue; **dec** – decrease; **foll** – following; **in** – inches; **inc** – increase; **K** – knit; **P** – purl; **patt** – pattern; **rem** – remaining; **rep** – repeat; **RS** – right side; **sl** – slip; **st(s)** – stitch(es); **st-st** – stocking stitch; **tog** – together; **WS** – wrong side. Work instructions in square brackets the number of times given.

FRONT
With 3¼mm needles and M, cast on 72 (78) sts. Work 16 rows in K 1, P 1 rib, inc 1 st at end of final row. (73 [79] sts.) Change to 4mm needles **. Cont in st-st from chart 1 thus: **1st row (RS):** reading row 1 of chart from right to left, rep 6 patt sts until 1 st remains, K st after dotted line. **2nd row:** reading row 2 of chart from left to right, P st before dotted line then rep 6 patt sts to end. **3rd to 14th rows:** as 1st and 2nd rows, working appropriate rows of chart. Cont in st-st from chart 2. Use separate short lengths of C for each back leg and for the front pair, carrying A loosely across WS when not in use. When working body and head, use separate balls of A for each side. Twist yarns tog on WS at each colour change to prevent holes. **1st row (RS):** K 27 (30) A, then reading chart from right to left, K 19 sts of row 1 of chart, K 27 (30) A. **2nd row:** P 27 (30) A, then reading chart from left to right, P 19 sts of row 2 of chart, P 27 (30 A). **3rd to 26th rows:** as 1st and 2nd rows, working appropriate rows of chart. K 1 row A. **Next row:** P 1 M, [1 A, 1 M] to end. Now work from chart 3 as given for chart 1. Rep the 14 rows of chart until front measures 26 (30cm) from cast-on edge, ending with a WS row. **Neck shaping: 1st row:** patt 28 (30) sts, turn. Cont on these sts only for 1st side. Keeping patt correct, dec 1 st at neck edge on every P row until 22 (24) sts rem, ending with a P row. **Shoulder shaping:** casts off 6 sts at beg of next row and on the foll 2 alt rows. Patt 1 row. Cast off rem 4 (6) sts. **Next row:** with RS facing, sl centre 17 (19) sts onto a stitch holder, rejoin yarn to inner end of rem 28 (30) sts and patt to end. Complete to match 1st side but work 1 row straight before working shoulder shaping.

BACK
Work as front to **. Cont in st-st in M until back measures the same as front to shoulders, ending with a P row. **Shoulder shaping:** cast off 6 sts at beg of next 6 rows and 4 (6) sts on the foll 2 rows. Leave rem 29 (31) sts on a stitch holder.

SLEEVES
With 3¼mm needles and M, cast on 30 (34) sts. Work 16 rows in K 1, P 1 rib. **Inc row:** P 4, [inc in next st, P 1] to end. (43 [49] sts.) Change to 4mm needles. Cont in st-st from chart 3 as given for front and inc 1 st at each end of 7th row and every foll 8th (10th) row until there are 55 (61) sts, working inc sts into patt. Patt straight until the sleeve measures approximately 26 (29)cm from cast-on edge, ending with a 4th or 10th row. Cast off.

NECKBAND
Join right shoulder seam. With RS facing, using 3¼mm needles and M, pick up and K 16 sts evenly down left front neck, K across 17 (19) sts at centre front, pick up and K 16 sts up right front neck then K across 29 (31) sts of back neck. (78 [82] sts.) Work 5cm in K 1, P 1 rib. Cast off.

TO MAKE UP
Join left shoulder and neckband seam. Fold neckband in half onto WS and catch stitch loosely in place. With centre of cast-off edge of sleeves to shoulder seams, sew on sleeves. Join side and sleeve seams.

HAT
With 3¼mm needles and A, cast on 103 sts. Work 6cm in K 1, P 1 rib, beg alt rows P 1. Change to 4mm needles. Cont in st-st. Work 22 rows. **Shape crown: 1st row:** K 1, K 2 tog, [K 7, K 2 tog] 11 times, K 1. Beg P, st-st 3 rows. **5th row:** [K 4, K 2 tog] to last st, K 1. Beg P, st-st 3 rows. **9th row:** [K 3, K 2 tog] to last st, K 1. P 1 row. **11th row:** [K 2, K 2 tog] to last st, K 1. P 1 row. **13th row:** [K1, K2 tog] to last st, K 1. P 1 row. **15th row:** [K 2 tog] to last st, K 1. P 1 row. **17th row:** [K 2 tog] to end. Break off yarn leaving sufficient yarn to join seam. Thread end through rem 8 sts, draw up securely and join centre-back seam. Make a pompon in M and sew firmly to top of hat.

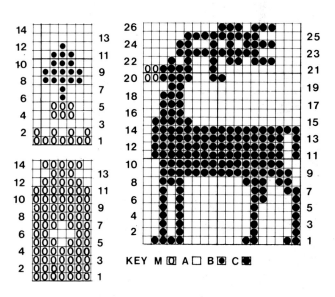

KEY M ▨ A ☐ B ◉ C ■

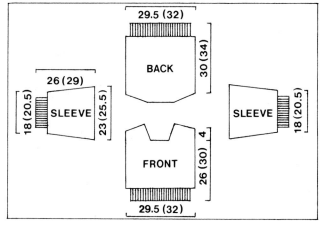

3
DECORATIONS AND CARDS

A HOUSE THAT'S FILLED WITH STUNNING DECORATIONS THAT YOU AND KIDS HAVE MADE YOURSELVES HAS THAT SPECIAL WELCOMING CHRISTMAS FLAVOUR. PILE THE TABLE HIGH WITH HOME-MADE DECORATIONS, ADORN A TREE WITH ANGELS AND SNOWFLAKES, OR MAKE A TRADITIONAL CHRISTMAS WREATH. FOR A CO-ORDINATED DESIGNER LOOK, CHOOSE A FAVOURITE COLOUR THEME FOR YOUR MAKES, OR LINK THE IDEAS BY DRESSING THEM UP WITH MATCHING RIBBONS. BRIGHTEN UP A FRIEND OR NEIGHBOUR'S MANTEL-PIECE TOO WITH OUR FUN RANGE OF HOME-MADE CHRIST-MAS CARDS. YOU DON'T NEED ANY SPECIAL SKILLS TO MAKE THEM, BUT IT HELPS TO HAVE A SHARP PAIR OF SCISSORS, A CRAFT KNIFE AND A RULER AT THE READY.

MAKING CONCERTINAS

1 Cut equal lengths of green and red giftwrap ribbon.

2 Place the ribbon at right angles and stick or staple the two ends together. Fold the green strip upwards.

3 Fold the red ribbon to the left.

4 Fold the green ribbon downwards.

5 Fold the red ribbon to the right. Continue until the strips of ribbon are used up – glue on new pieces if necessary.

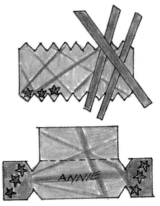

SANTA CENTREPIECE

Large yoghurt pot, plus lid
20cm (7¾in) of 140cm (55in) wide red polyester fleece
70mm (2¾in) craft ball
Thick polyester wadding scraps
Felt scraps in black and red
Scrap of gold cardboard
Glue
Tracing paper
Foil-wrapped chocolate coins

1 To make the body, cut out a 32 × 15cm (12½ × 6in) rectangle of fleece and wrap it around the yoghurt pot. Trim away the excess so that the fleece just covers the base of the pot, and glue into place. For the arms, cut out two strips of fleece, each measuring 6 × 7.5cm (2¼ × 3in). For the mittens, cut out two hand shapes from black felt. To assemble the arms, fold the long sides of the fleece strips to the centre and tuck the mittens inside. Glue into place. To make the cuffs, cut out two narrow strips of wadding and glue these to the base of the arms.

2 To make the head, turn the yoghurt pot upside down and glue the craft ball to the

bottom of the pot. Next, glue the arms into place. Trace off the hat template from p.59 and cut out a hat from red fleece. Glue the long edges of the hat together to form a cone and glue this to the head. Make a bobble from wadding and glue this to the top of the hat. Decorate the lower edge of the rim with wadding trimming. Next, cut out and glue on the felt eyes, eyebrows, nose and buttons. Glue a piece of wadding to the face for the beard. To make the belt, cut out a 30 × 2.5cm (12 × 1in) strip from black felt and a buckle shape from cardboard. Thread the buckle onto the felt belt and glue around Santa's waist.

3 Finally, fill the Santa with chocolates and replace the yoghurt pot lid.

NAPKIN RINGS AND PLACE CARDS

Green cardboard
Red sticky stars
Gold spray paint
Stapler and staples

1 To make a napkin ring, cut a 14 × 6.5cm (5½ × 2½in) rectangle from cardboard. Cut the long sides to a zigzag shape. Scatter strips of card along the top edge and spray gold. Remove the strips to reveal the green pattern and stick on the stars. Finally, staple the short ends together.

2 To make a place card, cut out the basic shape from cardboard using the diagram as a guideline. Decorate the card in the same way as the napkin ring and write on the name. Finally, fold down the top flap so that the place card stands up.

STAND-UP STARS

Cardboard
Scissors
Gold spray paint

1 Trace off the red template from p.59, then cut out two identical stars from cardboard using scissors. Spray both sides of the card with gold paint and leave to dry.

2 When the stars are fully dry, cut along the solid line of one and along the dotted lines of the other and slot the two stars together.

CONCERTINA NAPKIN RINGS

2cm (¾in) wide self-adhesive giftwrap ribbon in red and green

1 Cut out 35cm (13¾in) strips of green and red ribbon, and make into concertinas, following the instructions given opposite, then moisten the two ends and stick them together to form a ring.

2 Next, cut two more strips of ribbon – one green and one red – each measuring 10cm (4in) in length. Moisten and stick them together at one end. Trim the remaining ends to points and stick onto the concertina ring.

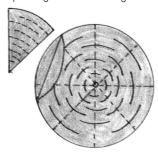

GLORIOUS GARLANDS

Green tissue paper
Red and green narrow giftwrap ribbon
Stapler and staples
Glue

1 Cut 80 circles, 12cm (4¾in) in diameter, from tissue paper and place them in sets of pairs.

2 To make the lanterns, fold 20 of the pairs into quarters, then fold one more time. Using the dotted lines in the diagram (below) for reference, make incisions in the paper and snip off the pointed end. Open out the circles and stick each pair together using spots of glue around the edges.

3 To make fans, fold the remaining 30 pairs of circles into quarters, then fold three times more. Using the diagram (below) for reference, cut out small incisions in the paper and snip off the end points. Open out.

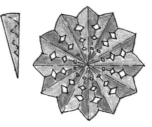

4 Cut a 3.7m (23ft) length of green ribbon. Thread this through the centre point of one of the pairs of fans. Fold each fan shape in half and staple the centre to the ribbon. Tie a small red ribbon bow onto the green ribbon between the folded backs of the fans. Next, thread on one of the lanterns. Open out. Staple each end to the ribbon. Continue assembling in this way until the garland is complete.

FLORAL TABLE DECORATIONS

Green and red crepe paper
2cm (¾in) wide self-adhesive ribbon in red and green
Narrow giftwrap ribbon in red and green
Stem wires and reel wire
Florists' tape
8cm (3¼in) diameter cylinder of oasis
Dressmaker's pins
Pine cones
Glue

1 For a large arrangement, cut out a 3cm (1¼in) slice of oasis. Make a concertina from 81.5cm (32in) lengths of self-adhesive ribbon. Glue the ends together. Pin the concertina around the outside of the oasis.

2 For decoration, make up eight flowers by winding a green crepe paper strip around the top of a piece of stem wire. For the petals, cut out a red crepe strip with jagged edges and wind this onto the stem. Add a ribbon loop. Secure the crepe and ribbon at the base of the petals with reel wire and then cover the wire stem with florists' tape.

3 Make up four more flowers in the same way, adding a crepe leaf and extra ribbon loops.

4 Next, make up two ribbon sprays by attaching two loops of ribbon to a piece of stem wire. Secure with reel wire and cover with florists' tape.

5 To wire the cones, hook some florists' wire onto the prongs of the cones and twist the ends together.

6 To assemble the table decorations, arrange the flowers around the oasis, tucking in the cones at intervals to fill in the gaps. Finally, add the ribbon sprays.

7 For a small arrangement, use a 3.2cm (1¼in) slice of oasis and cut this into three individual wedges. Make the concertinas from 50cm (19½in) lengths of ribbon and pin them around the oasis. Decorate with two flowers with leaves and ribbons, one ribbon spray and two wired cones. Assemble as before.

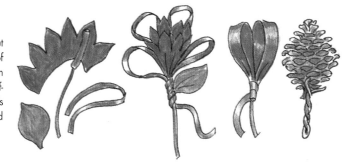

LARGE STAR

5 continental ice-cream cones
Stiff wire
White yarn
Dried flowers

1 To make the basic star shape, bend a length of stiff wire into a five-pointed shape.

2 Wind white yarn around the ice-cream cones and place a cone onto each wire prong.

3 Finally, insert a bunch of dried flowers into the centre of the star shape.

GINGERBREAD MEN

Brown cardboard
White paint
String

1 Draw around a gingerbread man cutter onto brown cardboard. Cut out the shapes and paint on the features.

2 Using a skewer, make a hole near the top of the head and make a loop from string for hanging.

PINE CONES

Pine cones
Fine florists' wire

1 Using florists' wire, bind the base of the cones with wire. Create a loop at the end for hanging and attach the wired cone to the tree.

CHRISTMAS COOKIES

Makes 30-32
325g (12oz) plain flour
1tsp bicarbonate of soda
2tsp ground ginger
100g (4oz) butter
150g (6oz) soft light-brown
  sugar
1 egg
4tbsp syrup
225g (8oz) icing sugar

1 Sift the flour with the bicarbonate of soda and ginger. Rub in the butter, and stir in the sugar.

2 Beat together the egg and syrup and add to the dry ingredients to form a soft dough.

Knead the dough until smooth.

3 Roll out the mixture to a thickness of 6mm (¼in). Using pastry cutters, cut out bell and holly shapes and place on a greased baking sheet. Using a skewer, make a hole near the top for hanging.

4 Bake at 190°C (375°F/ Gas 5) for 12 minutes or until golden. Leave to cool.

5 To make the icing, sift the icing sugar into a bowl and bind with a little water to form a stiff paste. Spread to within 6mm (¼in) of the edge of the shapes and leave to dry. Finally, thread with ribbon for hanging.

FLORAL BUNCHES

Twigs
Dried flowers
Raffia in assorted colours
Fine wire

1 Bind together short twigs or dried flowers with natural raffia to form small bundles.

2 Bind a piece of wire around the base and use this to attach the floral bunches to the tree.

TINY STARS

3 cups plain flour
1 cup salt
1 cup water
Paint or varnish
or cloves and glue

1 Mix the flour with the salt and bind the mixture together with water. Knead until smooth, then roll out and cut into star shapes using pastry cutters.

2 Place the shapes onto a baking sheet and make a small hole for hanging near the top. Leave to stand for 24 hours.

3 Bake at 100°C (200°F/ Gas ¼ for 2-3 hours.

4 Leave to cool and paint or varnish or decorate with glued-on cloves.

CORNUCOPIA

Continental ice-cream cones
Yarn in assorted colours or lace
  trimming
Dried flowers
Fine wire

1 First bind the yarn or lace around the cones in a spiral pattern.

2 Next, fill the inside of the cones with dried flowers. Pierce the top of each cone with a skewer and insert the wire through the hole. Twist the wire ends together to form a loop and use this to attach the cone to the tree.

tree MAGIC

WHITE STAR

30 × 20cm (12 × 8in) white
  cardboard
Scissors

1 Using the template on p.59,
cut out five shapes from white
cardboard. Using the point of
the scissors, score along
the broken lines.

2 To make up the star shape,
bring tab 1 to edge 1 and
glue together. Repeat five times for
each shape.

3 Assemble the star points by
sticking tab 2 of one piece
under edge 2 of the next piece,
and tab 3 under flat edge 3 of the
next piece.

HEARTS

Silver adhesive-backed plastic
White tissue paper
String or ribbon

1 Using the template on p.59,
cut two outlines of hearts in
silver plastic. Peel away the backing from one piece and stick it
onto white tissue paper. Turn the
paper over and stick the other
heart outline over the first, matching the edges.

2 Trim away the excess tissue
and decorate with silver
stars. Finally, pierce the top of the
heart with a skewer and thread
with string or ribbon.

SNOWFLAKES

White paper
Scissors

1 Fold a square of white paper
into quarters, then into
eighths. Snip away tiny portions
along the folds using small sharp
scissors.

2 Finally, open out the shape
to reveal a snowflake and
attach a loop for hanging.

DOVES

White cardboard
14 × 10cm (5½ × 4in) white
  paper

1 Using the template on p.59,
cut out a dove shape from
white cardboard.

2 Make 6mm (¼in) folds
across the width of the
paper and thread the resulting
concertinaed paper through the
slot in the dove. Fan out the
wings. Stick the wings together at
the top to make a fan shape.
Pierce the wings at the top for the
hanging loop.

ANGELS

Flesh-pink jersey fabric
20cm (7¾in) wide white ribbon
Broderie Anglaise
Toy filling
Felt hair
Embroidery thread
Blusher

1 Trace off the template from
p.59 and cut out two body
shapes from flesh-pink jersey fabric. With right sides together and
raw edges even, stitch the bodies
together leaving a gap for turning.
Turn through, stuff with toy filling
and slipstitch the opening.

2 To make the surplice, cut
out two 12cm (4¾in)
pieces of 8cm (3⅓in) wide
broderie Anglaise. Turn under
1cm (⅜in) to the wrong side
along the top edge. With right
sides together, stitch the side
seams to fit the body shape. Slip
the body into the dress.

3 To make the wings, fold the
ribbon in half and stitch it to
the back. Sew on the felt hair and
hanging loop, then embroider the
features and apply pink blusher to
the cheeks.

cracker CRAFT

FORMAL DRESSING

3 pieces of black adhesive-backed vinyl, measuring 16 × 9cm (6¼ × 3½ in) each
Party cracker
Lace for trimming
Silk flowers and holly for decoration

1 Peel away the backing from the three pieces of vinyl and stick these around the outside of the cracker, taking care to avoid creases.

2 Glue the lace to the ends and decorate the central barrel with real holly and silk flowers.

ALL GOLD

3 pieces of gold paper, each measuring 35 × 9cm (13¾ × 3½ in)
Party cracker
Scraps of gold paper

1 Pleat the gold paper and wrap it around the barrel and ends of the cracker. Glue in place.

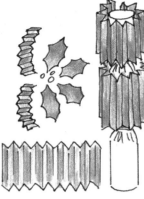

2 Cut out four holly leaves from the scraps of gold paper and use a pin to score down the centre of each to create a crease. Cut out a few narrow strips of gold paper and fold them into pleats. Stick the pleated strips, gold paper beads and pleated gold paper to the central barrel.

PURE FABRICATION

3 pieces of fabric, each measuring 16 × 11cm (6¼ × 4¼ in)

Party cracker
Narrow ribbon
Beads
Narrow parcel ribbon

1 Cover the barrel and ends of the cracker with the fabric, then neaten the raw ends by turning them under by 1cm (⅜ in) and securing them with glue.

2 Trim the edges with ribbon and decorate the central barrel with beads and swirls of ribbon, made by curling parcel ribbon over closed scissor blades.

GENTLEMAN'S RELISH

Festive wrapping paper
Party cracker
Pine cones, berries and leaves to decorate
Glue
Decorative braid

1 Cut out strips of wrapping paper large enough to cover the barrel and ends of the cracker. Glue these to the cracker, then trim the ends with decorative braid.

2 Using berries, pine cones and leaves, make up a small winter bouquet and glue this to the central barrel.

FLIGHTS OF FANTASY

70cm (27½ in) of 20cm (7¾ in) wide lace
Party cracker
Lace motif

1 Cut the lace in half to form two 35cm (13¾ in) long strips. Use a running stitch to gather one long side of each, one-third from the edge. Draw up the gathers and tie a lace frill around each end of the cracker. Using adhesive, glue a lace motif to the centre.

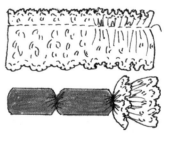

We bought an inexpensive box of crackers, re-used the cardboard, snaps, mottoes and hats, and added personal gifts too. Follow these steps for the basic shape.

1 Take apart a cracker and smooth out the wrapper. Using this as a template, cut out a new piece of crepe paper, making sure that the long sides are parallel to the grain.

2 Cut a piece of thin paper 2cm (¾ in) smaller for the lining. Place the motto, hat and present inside the inner tube. Put the lining paper over the crepe paper and place the snap and the tube in the centre.

3 Wind the paper around the tube and glue into place. To hold the shape together, slip a toilet-roll tube into the cracker ends, then tie a piece of thread around the crepe paper between the tubes. Finally, remove the outer tubes.

IVY CENTREPIECE

25-cm (9¾-in) diameter florists' foam ring with plastic holder
Variegated ivy
Medium stub wires from florist
Holly
Silk flowers
Small ribbon bows
Small double-sided sticky pads
25cm (9¾in) round, thin cake board
Candles
Modelling clay

1 First dampen the foam ring with water. Next, wind lengths of ivy around the ring, pushing the stems into the foam to secure them. Bend the stub wires into hairpin shapes and use these to secure the ivy in place.

2 Next, push sprigs of holly into the ring and tuck artificial flowers and bows among the foliage.

3 Using sticky pads, secure the ring to the cake board.

4 Finally, trim the candles to different lengths and stick them firmly to the cake board using modelling clay.

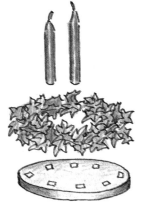

rings
AND WREATHS

NATURAL WREATH

25.5cm (10in) willow wreath base
String
Medium stub wires from florist
Assorted dried flowers, cereals, berries, ornamental seedheads and pine cones

1 Before you start assembling the wreath, attach a string loop to the willow base for hanging. Trim away the stems of the dried flowers and seedheads to 6cm (2¼in) and then strengthen them by binding them with stem wire. Next, bind the base of the pine cones with stub wire.

2 Attach the large dried flowers to the wreath by pushing their wire stems firmly into the base. Arrange the brighter flowers around the centre to give the design depth, then tuck the teasels and cereals into the base. Decorate the outside edges with honesty which will glimmer in the light.

3 Fill in any gaps between the larger items with small clusters of flowers and finally add the berries.

TRADITIONAL CHRISTMAS RING

Wire coathanger
Branches of evergreens – e.g.
  yew, cypress, ivy, variegated
  periwinkle, holly
Medium stub wires from florist
Fabric flowers
String of gold beads
2m (6½ ft) narrow green ribbon
2m (6½ ft) wide red ribbon

1 Bend the hanger into a ring shape and twist the ends together to secure them. First attach feathery evergreens – such as yew and cypress – then attach the ivy to the ring using stem wires. Next, wire together small sprigs of periwinkle and holly and fasten them to the ring in the same way.

2 Wind the string of beads around the wreath, tucking in the silk flowers as you wind. Tie some 50cm (19½ in) lengths of green ribbon onto the beads at intervals in bows. Finally, make the red ribbon into a bow and fasten it to the top of the wreath.

card TRICKS

FABULOUS PHOTOCOPIES

A4 paper
Old Christmas cards
Coloured cardboard
Old newspaper

Before you begin, make sure that your cards are out of copyright. Copyright ends 50 years after death of an artist, or after first publication of a photograph.

Note: you should be able to gain access to a photocopier at a local library or print shop.

1 Fold a piece of A4 paper in half. Photocopy an old Christmas card onto a sheet of white A4 paper, positioning it so that the picture forms the front when the card is folded. Next, photocopy the master copy onto coloured paper. Highlight a special part of the picture with a felt-tip pen.

2 To make the Christmas crackers, fold a sheet of A4 paper in half lengthways. Using our picture for reference, draw a cracker shape onto cardboard, cut it out and place it on the folded paper. Cut out individual letters from an old newspaper and stick them between the cracker to form a message. Remove the cracker and copy the master greeting message onto coloured paper. Finally, stick the cracker shapes onto each card.

WINDOW WONDERLANDS

Cardboard in assorted colours·
Tracing paper
Craft knife
Photograph or Christmas card
Glue
Ribbon

1 To make the Georgian window, trace off the template (right) and enlarge it on a photocopier until it measures 15cm (6in) in height. Cut out two pieces of cardboard, each measuring 22 × 15cm (8½ × 6in), then mount the picture on one of these. On the second piece, score vertical fold lines, one in the middle and the other 1.3cm (½in) from each side. Transfer the tracing and trace again onto the cardboard to produce a complete window shape. Cut away the panes with a craft knife. Glue the front card to the back at the sides, then bend along the scored lines to make the card stand up. Glue holly and berries shapes to the corner.

2 To make the doors, cut a piece of cardboard twice the width and length of your picture, then stick the picture in the centre. Fold in the card edges to cover the photograph. Trace off the template (right) and trace one window design onto each side of the card. Open out the card and cut away the panes with a craft knife. Cut a wreath and berries out of card, glue the berries onto the wreath and attach the wreath to the door by passing a piece of ribbon through the wreath and window pane and tying it at the front in a bow. Finally, cut out and glue on a knocker, letterbox and milk bottles.

PRETTY IN PRINT

FOR THE ANGELS:

Saucer filled with white poster paint

Blue cardboard folded in half

Felt-tip pens

Scrap paper

Foil scraps

FOR THE KINGS:

Yellow cardboard, folded in half

Craft knife

Silver star

Waxed crayons

Marker pens

1 To make the angels (left), dip your thumb into the saucer of paint, blot it on scrap paper, then print by pressing your thumb down on the cardboard. Leave to dry, then draw on the features with a felt-tip pen. Make haloes by cutting out and sticking on scraps of foil. Finally, use a marker pen to draw on the clouds.

2 To make the three kings stencil, draw the basic body shape onto a piece of cardboard and cut out the cloak, head and crown with a craft knife. Place this stencil on the card and colour in the central areas with crayons. Cut out and glue on a blue shape for the sky, then stick on a silver star.

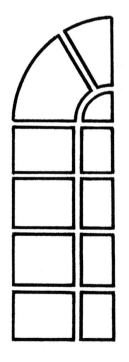

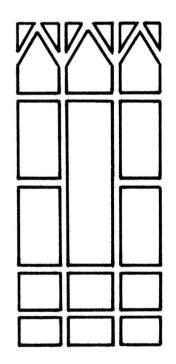

CHRISTMAS CUT-OUTS

FOR THE TREE:

Cardboard

Craft knife

Pencil

FOR THE STAR:

Cardboard in two colours

Craft knife

Glitter

Glue

1 To make the tree, cut out a rectangle measuring 19 × 25cm (7½ × 9¾in) from cardboard and fold it in half. On the front side, draw half a Christmas tree shape and cut it out through both layers to produce a complete Christmas tree. Open out. Next, use a pencil to draw a half tree shape 1.3cm (½in) from the outer edge of the first Christmas tree and cut along the pencil line with a craft knife, this time making sure that you only cut through one thickness. Finally, push out the resulting cut-out shape and stand the card up.

2 To make the star, cut out a piece of cardboard measuring 20 × 30.5 cm (7¾ × 12in). Mark parallel lines 5cm (2in), then 12.5cm (5in) from each end. Draw a half star shape onto each end and cut out. Fold each star shape back on itself. Next, cut out two panels from a contrasting coloured cardboard, each measuring 5 × 20cm (2 × 7¾in), and stick one behind each star shape. Write a message on the inside of the card, then spread with glue and sprinkle with glitter. Allow to dry.

4

KIDS' CRAFTS

KIDS CAN'T RESIST GETTING INVOLVED WITH CRAFTS, PARTIC-
ULARLY IF YOU SET THEM THEIR VERY OWN PROJECTS.
THEY'LL HAPPILY WHILE AWAY HOURS MAKING TREE-LOADS
OF DECORATIONS, CARDS AND PRESENTS, LEAVING YOU
MORE TIME TO GET ORGANIZED. START THEM OFF ON A
CAREER OF STITCHING, STICKING AND MOULDING WITH THESE
MAKES, WHICH WERE ALL SPECIALLY CHOSEN AND DESIGNED
TO SUIT SMALL HANDS. BEGIN A PRODUCTION LINE AND
WATCH THE PILE GROW – IT'S SURE TO SAVE ON BUYING
EXPENSIVE DECORATIONS AND CHRISTMAS TREATS.

festive FUN

WRAP IT UP

To make the decorated wrapping papers shown here, you will need a basic kit which comprises:

Lining paper

Powder paints, ready-mixed and stored in screw-top jars

Assorted brushes

● Mix each colour in a screw-top jar so that any left-over paint can be used again.

● Use a different paintbrush for each colour.

● Always work on a well-protected table and cover the floors as well if necessary.

● Choose Christmas colours that go well together, such as red and green, purple and blue, or red and black.

● If you want to make matching gift tags, paint them at the same time as the paper.

★ ★ ★

SPLITTER SPLATTER

Basic kit (see above)

Jam jars

Paper

1 Dip a paintbrush into the paint jar in order to cover the bristles completely with paint.

2 Hold the brush with the bristles angled downward. Using just your fingertips, flick the bristles in the direction of the paper, so that the paint splatters all over it.

3 Keep flicking until the paint runs out, then reload the brush with paint and start again. Make sure that you use a different brush and clean hands for each colour.

PRETTY BUBBLES

Powdered paints in various colours

225g (8oz) margarine tub for each paint colour

Washing-up liquid

Drinking straws

Paper

Water

1 Put 3tbsp powder paint into a tub. Add enough water to the paint so that the mixture resembles single cream in consistency, then add a squeeze of washing-up liquid.

2 Put in a straw and blow gently into the liquid (don't suck) until the surface bubbles reach high above the top of the tub and start to overflow.

3 Remove the straw and place a section of paper lightly down on the bubbles. Lift off the paper and repeat the process with another section of paper until the whole sheet is covered with bubble prints. Repeat the process with different coloured paints for a multi-coloured effect.

RAG TIME

(7+ years)

Basic kit (above left)

Clean cotton rag, twisted or folded into a shape

A helper

1 Paint a sheet of paper all over in one colour and leave to dry.

2 Working in pairs, take a wide paintbrush and put a blob of contrasting paint near the left-hand edge of the paper. Then using a paintbrush, paint a 15cm (6in) wide strip along the length of the paper. As the first person paints the strip, the second person needs to roll the cotton rag along the strip to create a textured pattern. The rag will pick up a lot of the wet paint, leaving an interesting pattern as it reveals some of the original colour beneath.

3 Next drop another contrasting blob of paint beside the first colour and draw a second strip alongside it. Repeat this process until the entire sheet is covered. Meanwhile, the one with the rag should keep rolling over each fresh strip, refolding the cloth each time to prevent smudging (so that you always roll with a dry bit). Note: both of you will have to work fast as the paint dries very quickly.

FLAKED OUT

(7+ years)

Basic kit (above left) without brushes

2 pieces of plain paper, 20cm (8in) square

2 round pieces of plain paper, 15cm (6in) in diameter

Lining paper

Scissors

Paperclips

Sponge

1 Fold all the squares and circles in half, fold in half again, then fold in half a third time.

2 Cut small shapes (squares and circles) out of the folded edges. Note: you will only need to cut "half" the shape since it will be full-sized when it is opened out – i.e. if you cut a semi-circular shape, it will end up as a circle.

3 Unfold the papers, which should now resemble snowflakes. Lay one on the lining paper and use a paperclip to secure it in place. Dip the sponge in paint and sponge over the snowflake so that the colour seeps through the holes and onto the paper beneath. Then unclip the snowflake and carefully lift it off. Turn the snowflake over and press it down on another area of paper so that the reverse pattern transfers to the paper. Repeat these processes using different coloured paints and freshly cut snow-flakes.

PLAYING MARBLES

Old roller-paint tray or small roasting tin

3 small tins of enamel paint (as used for model kits), e.g. blue, yellow and silver, or green, gold and red

Lining paper

1 Fill the tray or roasting tin almost to the top with cold water.

2 Add a few drops of each of the paints and stir gently in order to break up any large areas of colour. As the paint is oil-based it will not mix with the water but instead lies on the surface in swirls.

3 Carefully place one section of the paper over the tray and press it down gently onto the water and paint mixture, then lift off.

4 Repeat the process, placing another section of the paper on the liquid each time in order to repeat the pattern.

SWEET LANTERNS

Red cardboard
Scissors
Sweets
Plastic kitchen film
Stapler and staples

1 Trace off the template from p.60 and use this to cut out a shape from cardboard. Using the solid vertical lines in the diagram for reference, cut even slits along the length of the cardboard.

2 Wrap a handful of sweets in plastic kitchen film and staple them to the top of the lantern.

3 Fold the sides of the lantern, as shown by the broken lines in the illustration, and staple the two narrow edges together to form a cylinder. Finally, make a handle by cutting out a narrow strip of paper and stapling it to either side of the top edge.

TREE TREATS

Coloured wrapping paper
Narrow cord or ribbon
Adhesive tape
Stapler
Adhesive-backed stars

1 Cut a large circle from coloured wrapping paper.

2 Fold it into 16ths and snip out two small triangles from the open side. Open out the shape, then refold it to form a tree shape (as shown in the diagram).

3 Pierce a hole in the top for hanging and thread through a cord or ribbon loop. Attach the loop to the inside using adhesive tape.

4 Staple the lower edges together and decorate the base with adhesive-backed stars. Finally, add a ribbon bow at the top for decoration.

PARTY POUCHES

Cardboard
Scissors
Double-sided adhesive tape
Foil-wrapped chocolates
Cord or ribbon

1 Using the template on p.60, cut out the basic shape from cardboard and score along the dotted lines using the point of a pair of closed scissors.

2 Apply double-sided adhesive tape to the flap, fill with chocolates or Christmas treats and stick the box together.

3 Using a skewer, punch two holes in the top of the cardboard pouch.

4 Finally, attach a cord or ribbon loop for hanging.

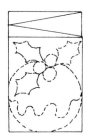

CONCERTINA CARDS

Cardboard
Marker pens
Felt scraps
Glue

1 Cut out a 31 × 12cm (12¼ × 4¾in) strip of cardboard. Fold it in half, then fold each half back again.

2 Draw a design on the front, making sure that it reaches to the side edges of the folded card (see diagram). Cut out the shape, colour in the features using marker pens and decorate with felt scraps.

SNOW MOBILE

White cardboard
61cm (24in) dress boning or plastic strip
Enamel paint
Marker pens
Paintbrush
Cord
Gold cardboard

1 Trace off the snowman template from p.61 and cut out eight snowmen shapes from white cardboard. Draw on the features using marker pens, then cut a slit in the lower half of four of the snowmen, starting at the base and finishing in the middle. Slot the four slit snowmen into the remaining four and make a hole near the top of each for hanging. Thread with cord.

2 Cut two lengths of dress boning or plastic strip, each measuring 30.5cm (12in), and coat in enamel paint. Pierce holes at either end of each piece and make one hole in the middle. Thread a snowman through each

of the end holes and fasten with a knot.

3 Cut out a star shape from gold cardboard, thread with cord and attach it to the middle hole. Next, join the two boning strips together by passing a piece of cord through both central holes and securing at the base with a large knot.

PRESENTATION CARDS

Coloured cardboard
Ribbon
Adhesive tape

1 Cut out a rectangle measuring 20 × 10cm (7¾ × 4in) from cardboard. Fold it in half, then cut a small slot in the middle of the fold for securing the ribbon.

2 Thread the ribbon through the slot and tie parcel fashion around the front of the card, finishing with a bow in the middle. Secure the ribbon in places with adhesive tape. Cut out a tag shape from cardboard and write on a message, then tuck it underneath the bow and secure with adhesive.

BOOTY BAGS

FOR ONE PUDDING:
Brown felt
White felt
Scraps of firm iron-on interfacing
Scraps of double-sided iron-on
    adhesive webbing
Ribbon
Clear glue
Glitter
Button
Needle
Thread

1 Using the template on p.61, cut out two circles in brown felt and two more in iron-on interfacing. Iron a piece of interfacing onto each of the brown felt circles.

2 Following the manufacturer's instructions, iron the adhesive webbing onto the white felt. From this, cut out a pair of white "creams". Remove the backing paper from the reverse and iron a cream onto each brown felt circle.

3 Cut a slit in one of the puddings to act as a buttonhole, then stitch a piece of ribbon to either side to create a loop for hanging.

4 With wrong sides together and raw edges even, blanket stitch the puddings together around the lower, brown sections. Sew on a button behind the buttonhole. Finally, spread glue over

the pudding and sprinkle with glitter. Leave to dry.

FOR ONE STOCKING:
Felt in assorted colours
Brass curtain ring
Needle and thread

1 Following the template on p.61, cut out two stocking shapes from felt, then cut out a felt strip measuring 8.5 × 1.3cm (3⅓ × ½in). Slip a brass curtain ring onto the felt strip and fold the strip in half.

2 With wrong sides together, stitch the two stocking shapes together using an even running stitch, making sure that you also enclose the two ends of the hanging strip in the seam.

FELT DECORATIONS

Felt in assorted colours
Tracing paper
Sequins
Narrow ribbon
Needle and thread

1 Fold a piece of tracing paper in half and place the fold of

the paper along the dotted line of the bell template on p.61. Repeat this process for each of the other shapes. Draw around and cut out the shapes. Next cut out two shapes for each design from felt. Open out, then stitch sequins onto one side of each shape.

2 With wrong sides together and raw edges even, blanket stitch the shapes together in pairs, making sure that you leave a gap in the top for tucking in a surprise chocolate. Finally, stitch on a piece of ribbon at the top to make a bow for hanging.

ANIMAL MAGIC

Felt squares in assorted colours
Felt scraps
Needle and thread

1 Trace off the template from p.59 and cut out two body pieces for each puppet in felt. With wrong sides together and raw edges even, stitch

both of the body pieces together.

2 Finally, cut out and stitch on the felt features, as shown in the illustrations below.

CHRISTMAS DOLL

71 × 71cm (28 × 28in) white satin lining

40.5cm (16in) of 6mm (¼in) wide lace

25cm (9¾in) of 1m (39in) wide gold net

3m (9¾ft) strung "pearls"

2 press studs

40.5 × 40.5cm (16 × 16in) plain cardboard

Gold spray paint

Fabric glue

Gold star sequins

Scrap of cardboard

Cocktail stick

Doll

Needle and thread

1 To make the dress, cut out a rectangle from white satin, measuring 25.5 × 48cm (10 × 18¾in). Hem the edges, then stitch lace along the two shortest edges. Next, sew on a 2cm (¾in) strip of gold net just behind each piece of lace (see main picture). With a short edge at the top, wrap the material around the doll, under her arms, overlapping at the back and secure with a few stitches at the top. Leave a 9cm (3½in) slit at the bottom.

2 To make the cape, draw a full-size paper pattern of the cape template, shown on p.61, and cut it out in white satin. Cut a neck opening for the head near the top edge and hem the edges. Stitch pearls around the neck opening, then sew a row of beads along the hem of the cape on both sides. Sew two press studs on the right side of the cape, where marked. Put the cape over the doll's head and stitch the neck hole almost closed.

3 Using the template on p.61 as a guideline, cut out the wings from cardboard and spray them with gold paint. Then cut two wing shapes from gold netting and use them to cover both sides of the wings. Secure with fabric glue. Stitch on the other sides of the press studs as shown.

4 For the finishing touches, tie the hair back from the face with a length of gold net. Glue sequins onto the clothes and wing tips and tuck some into the hair. Next, cut a small star from cardboard, glue it onto a cocktail stick and spray with gold paint. Fix the star banner in the doll's hand using adhesive tape. Press the wings in place on the cape and place the finished doll on top of the Christmas tree.

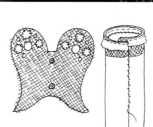

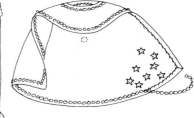

LIGHT SHOW

Modelling clay
Small cutter
Night light

1 Roll out the modelling clay and cut out a 5cm (2in) round base and a 6in (15cm) strip for the sides.

2 From the side piece, cut out star-shaped windows using a small cutter. If you are making a house, cut out square window shapes. To create a ridged roof, add more pieces of clay and build up the sides. Stick the sides around the base and press into place. Leave to dry.

3 When the clay is fully dry, insert a small night light.

RINGS

Salt dough (see below left)
Ribbon

1 Roll out three pieces of salt dough into "sausage" shapes and plait them together. Join the ends together to form a circle. Cut out some small flower and leaf shapes and use them to decorate the salt-dough wreath.

2 Leave the wreath to dry for a couple of days, before baking at 100°C (200°F/Gas ¼) for 2-3 hours. When the wreath is cool, add a ribbon for hanging.

TILES

Modelling clay
Craft knife
Teaspoon
Poster paints
Varnish

1 Roll out a ball of modelling clay and cut it into an even square shape using a craft knife. Next, using the end of a teaspoon, draw a wintery scene onto the moist surface of the tile or create a raised picture by sticking on small fragments of clay. Leave to dry overnight (refer to clay manufacturers' instructions).

2 Finally, colour in the features using poster paints and seal your design with a thin layer of varnish.

MAGNETS

Salt dough (see below left) or modelling clay
Badge bar or magnet
Plain cutter
Glue

1 Roll out the salt dough or clay and cut into Christmassy shapes using a plain cutter. Decorate with small holly or berry details (see picture). Leave to dry and, if necessary, bake in the oven (see manufacturer's instructions).

2 When the shapes are fully dry, glue on a badge bar or magnet.

SALT DOUGH

3 cups plain flour
1 cup salt
1 cup water

1 Mix the flour and the salt in a bowl, then stir in the water. Knead together until smooth. Cut into individual shapes and leave to dry out for a day or two. Once fully dry, bake in an oven at 100°C (200°F/Gas ¼) for 2-3 hours.

MARZIPAN ANIMAL MAGIC

Makes 20 assorted animals

1 × 500g (1.1lb) packet white
  marzipan
Green, red, yellow, pink and
  black food colouring
50g (2oz) icing sugar
1 red liquorice boot lace

1 Divide the marzipan into four equal portions – one for the crocodiles, one for the mice, one for the chicks and one for the elephants – and shape into animals (see below).

CROCODILES

Makes 4

1 First reserve a small ball of white marzipan for the eyes and teeth, then colour the remainder with green food colouring. Cut the green marzipan into four equal pieces.

2 From each quarter, reserve a little for the legs, then shape the remainder into 7.5cm (3in) bodies, tapering the ends to form a tail. Mould the reserved green marzipan into leg shapes and press onto the bodies.

3 For the mouth, create a slit in the blunt end of each body and insert a small ball of white marzipan. Using a knife, make indentations in the white marzipan to resemble teeth. Roll out eight small balls of white marzipan for the eyes and press them gently into place. Finally, mark crocodile scales across the back of each animal with the back of a knife.

MICE

Makes 6

1 Using pink food colouring, colour the marzipan pink. Reserve a small ball for the ears, then divide the remainder into six equal portions.

2 Mould each portion into a mouse shape, roll out two small balls of marzipan for the ears of each, flatten and press into place.

3 Mix the icing sugar with a little water and use it to pipe a small, white dot on the end of each nose (see Chicks, below). Finally, cut the liquorice boot lace into tiny pieces and press two strips onto the icing noses for whiskers.

CHICKS

Makes 5

1 Using red food colouring, colour a little of the marzipan red (this will be used for the beak and comb). Colour the remainder yellow, then divide into six portions. Dust your worksurface lightly with icing sugar and roll out one section, then cut it into 10 wing shapes.

2 Divide each of the remaining five sections into two, and shape into two balls – one for the head and one for the body – making sure that one is slightly smaller than the other. Pinch the larger ball in order to make a tail, then press a small ball on top. Next, press two wings onto each body.

3 Roll out the red marzipan and cut it into small diamond shapes and press onto the heads to form a comb and beak. Mix some icing sugar with a little water to form a smooth paste, then spoon into a greaseproof-paper piping bag. Snip off the end and pipe two small dots onto each bird to form the eyes.

ELEPHANTS

Makes 5

1 Using black food colouring, colour all the marzipan grey, then cut into six portions. Divide five of the portions in half and shape into five 6.5cm (2½in) "sausage" body shapes and five round heads. Make a slit at either end of each "sausage" and open out to form the legs. Curve the back of each "sausage" to form the body.

2 Shape the reserved ball into five trunk shapes and ten ear shapes. Press a trunk onto each of the bodies, and press two ears onto each of the heads. Using white icing sugar (see Chicks, below left) pipe white dots for the eyes.

POSH PEPPERMINT CREAMS

Makes 800g (1¾lb)

FOR THE SWEETS:
2 egg whites
½ tsp peppermint
  essence
550g (1¼lb) sifted icing sugar
Pink and green food colouring
225g (8oz) plain dark chocolate
TO SERVE:
4 paper doilies
4 shallow cheese-spread boxes

1 Put the egg whites and peppermint essence into a bowl and gradually beat in the icing sugar to form a smooth, stiff paste. Divide the mixture into two, and, using food colouring, colour one half green and one half pink.

2 Lightly dust your worksurface with icing sugar and roll out each half to a 23cm (9in) square. Place the pink square on top of the green square and press the two lightly together. Cut in half lengthways, then put one half on top of the other to form four layers. Press together. Cut the peppermint "cake" into 2cm (¾in) strips, then cut the strips into squares, triangles and bars. Place on greaseproof paper and leave to set.

3 Melt the chocolate in a bowl set over a pan of simmering water. Divide the peppermint creams into two portions and, using a fork, dip half of them in chocolate, leaving the other half plain. Once dipped, place the chocolate-coated peppermints on greaseproof paper and chill until set.

4 To serve, cut 2.5cm (1in) strips from the edges of four paper doilies. Stick these round the edges of four shallow cheese-spread boxes and decorate with ribbon. Finally, put the peppermint creams into *petits-fours* cases and arrange them in the boxes. Wrap with plastic kitchen film.

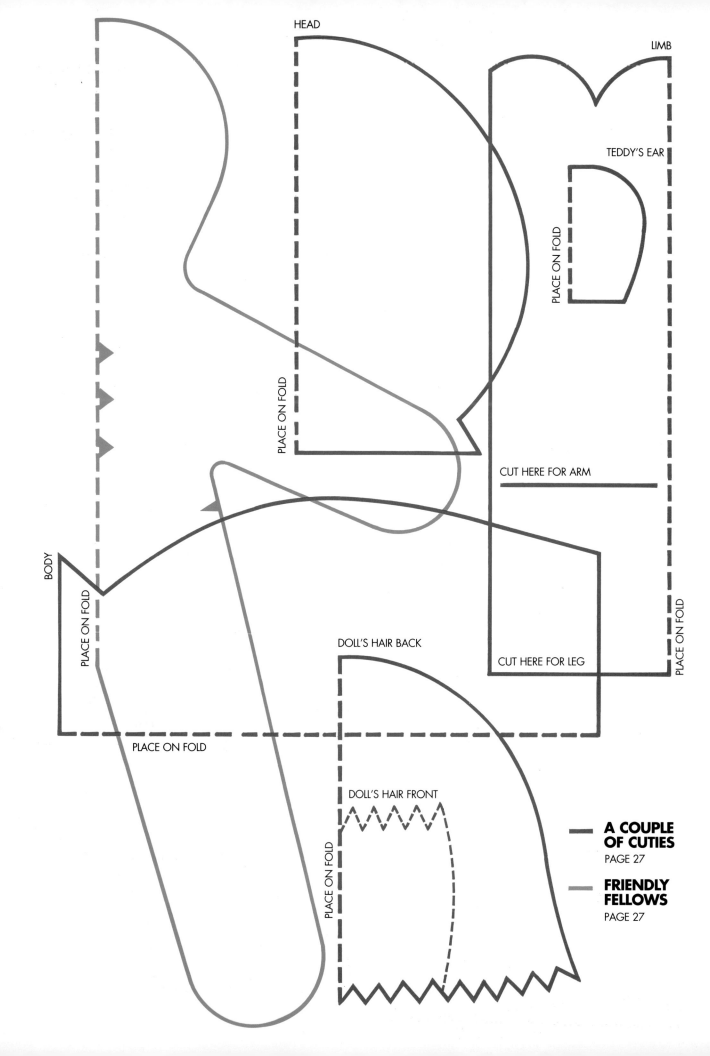

HEAD

LIMB

TEDDY'S EAR

PLACE ON FOLD

PLACE ON FOLD

CUT HERE FOR ARM

BODY

PLACE ON FOLD

PLACE ON FOLD

DOLL'S HAIR BACK

CUT HERE FOR LEG

PLACE ON FOLD

DOLL'S HAIR FRONT

PLACE ON FOLD

A COUPLE OF CUTIES
PAGE 27

FRIENDLY FELLOWS
PAGE 27

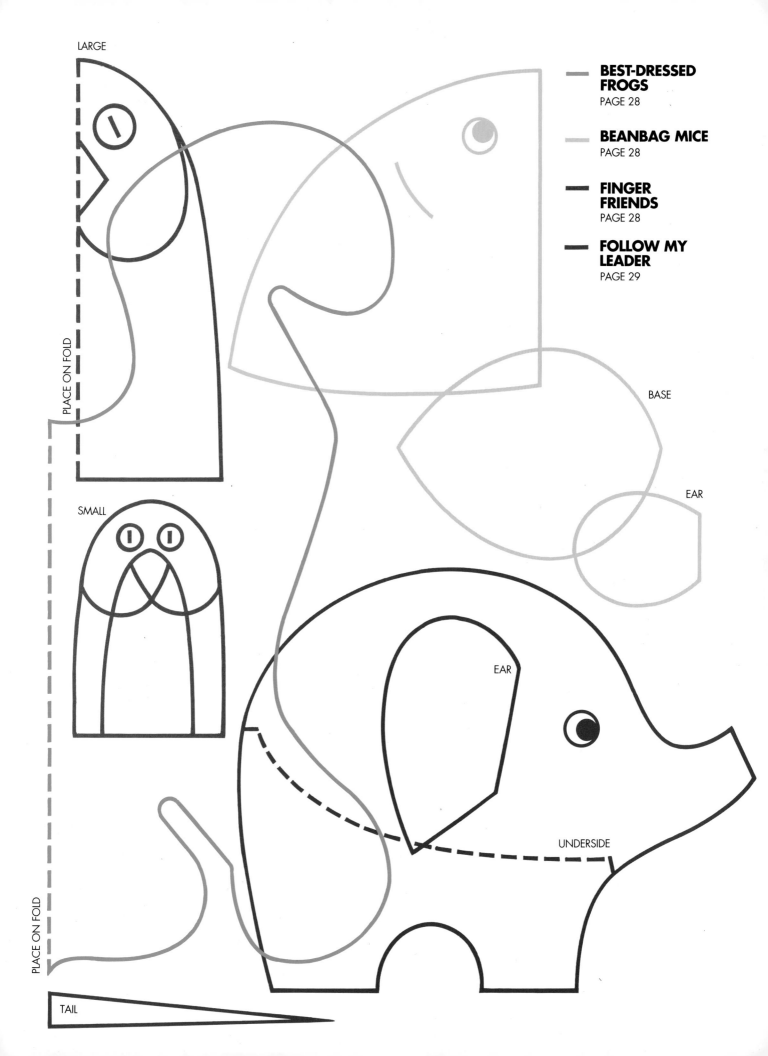

LARGE

PLACE ON FOLD

SMALL

PLACE ON FOLD

TAIL

BASE

EAR

EAR

UNDERSIDE

BEST-DRESSED
FROGS
PAGE 28

BEANBAG MICE
PAGE 28

FINGER
FRIENDS
PAGE 28

FOLLOW MY
LEADER
PAGE 29

BRONTO C HEAD

NECK FRILL

A & B BODY TOP

FIN

PLACE ON FOLD

C BODY TOP

UNDERBODY

**BRONTOSAURUS
BEAN BAGS**
PAGE 29

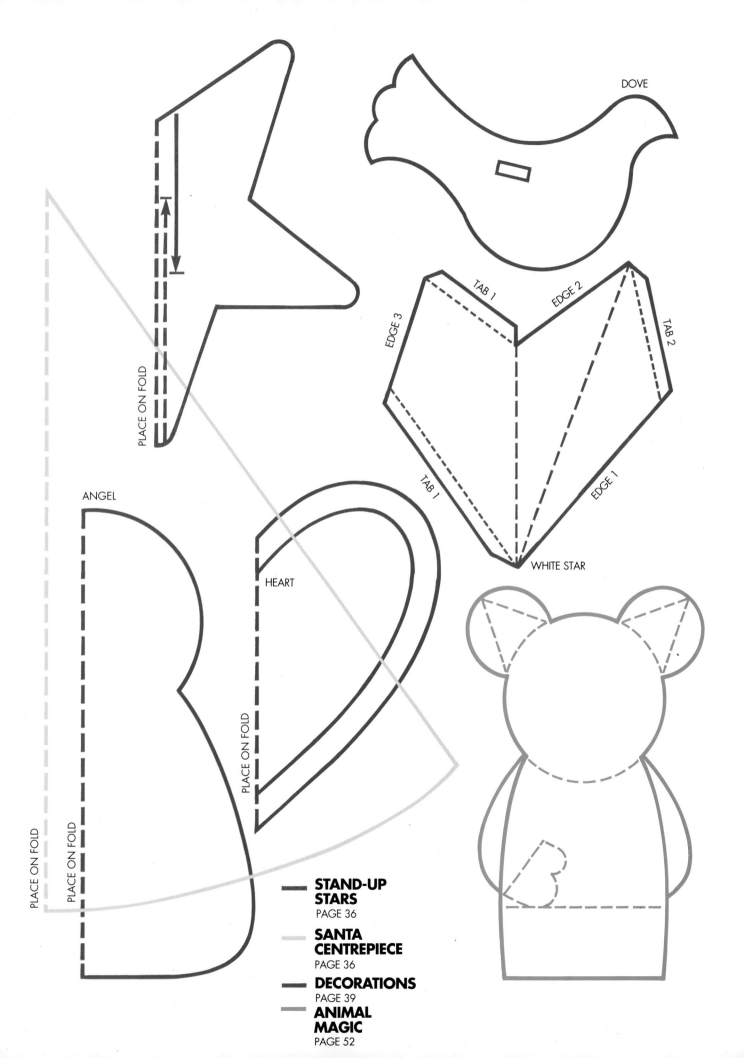

DOVE

PLACE ON FOLD

TAB 1 EDGE 2

EDGE 3

TAB 2

TAB 1

EDGE 1

WHITE STAR

ANGEL

HEART

PLACE ON FOLD

PLACE ON FOLD

PLACE ON FOLD

PLACE ON FOLD

STAND-UP STARS
PAGE 36

SANTA CENTREPIECE
PAGE 36

DECORATIONS
PAGE 39

ANIMAL MAGIC
PAGE 52

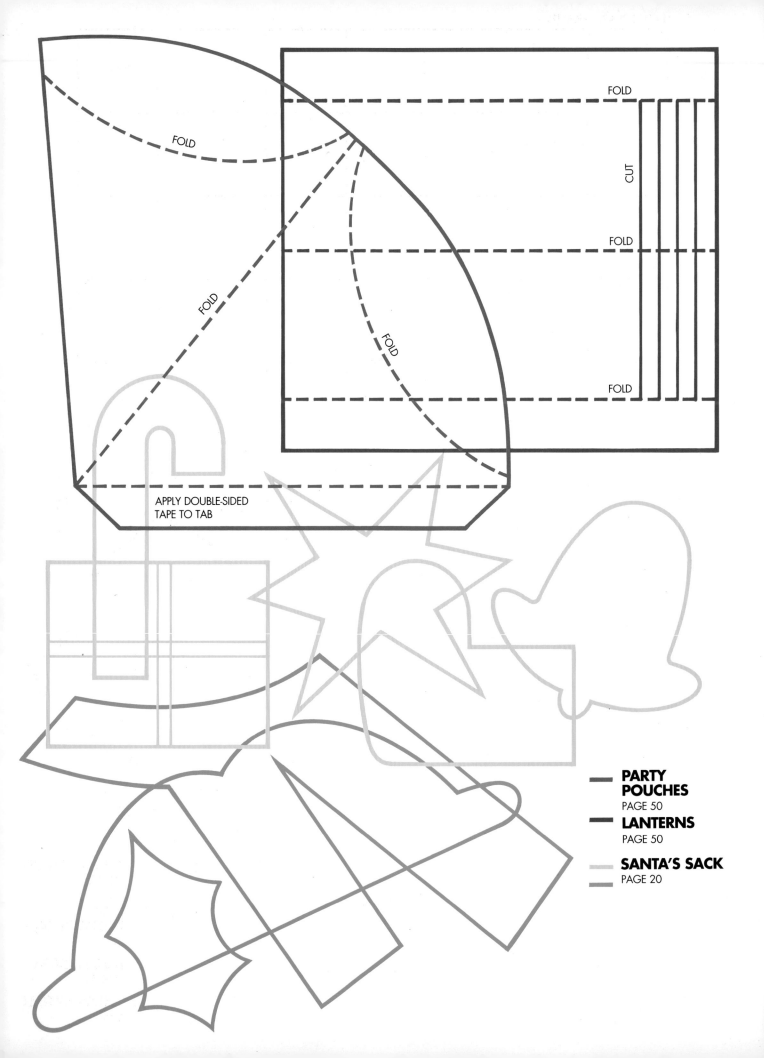

FOLD

FOLD

CUT

FOLD

FOLD

FOLD

FOLD

APPLY DOUBLE-SIDED
TAPE TO TAB

**PARTY
POUCHES**
PAGE 50

LANTERNS
PAGE 50

SANTA'S SACK
PAGE 20

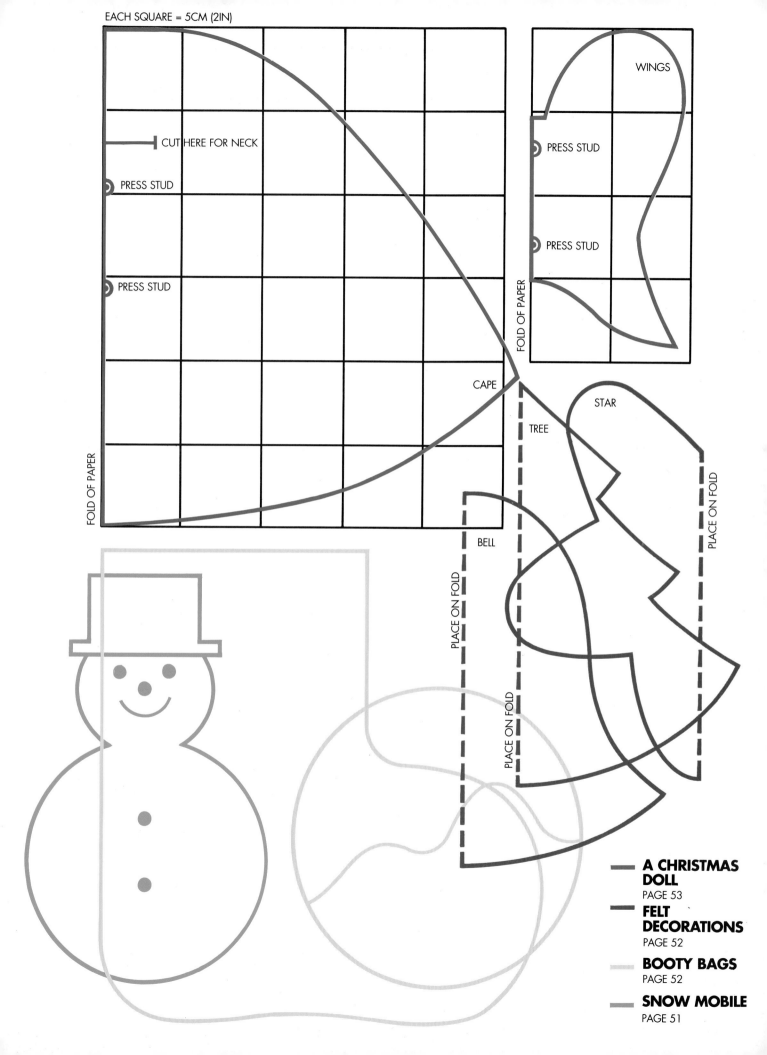

EACH SQUARE = 5CM (2IN)

CUT HERE FOR NECK

PRESS STUD

PRESS STUD

FOLD OF PAPER

CAPE

WINGS

PRESS STUD

PRESS STUD

FOLD OF PAPER

STAR

TREE

BELL

PLACE ON FOLD

PLACE ON FOLD

PLACE ON FOLD

A CHRISTMAS DOLL
PAGE 53

FELT DECORATIONS
PAGE 52

BOOTY BAGS
PAGE 52

SNOW MOBILE
PAGE 51

INDEX

ACKNOWLEDGMENTS

The photographs for this edition were supplied by Family Circle by John Cook.

The publishers would like to thank the following individuals for their generous help in producing this book: Maggi Altham, Lauren Floodgate and Caroline Rodrigues at Family Circle; Janette Hutchinson, Alison Jenkins, Cheryl Owen, Maggie Stevenson, Ann Stringer, Caroline Sullivan, Jill Visser and Judy Williams; Prue Bucknall for preparing the illustrations; Kuo Kang Chen for drawing the templates; and Judy Walker for proof-reading and indexing.